Racism by Proxy

Are you biased?

Am I?

The short answer is yes. We *all* are.

Having bias isn't a choice. We can't avoid it. We prefer members of our religion, our country, our political party, and speakers of our native language. We're taught bias unintentionally by people who aren't conscious of their biases, and we in turn unintentionally pass them on to others.

So it's not a "sin" to be biased. It's inevitable.

What matters is not allowing our unchosen biases to exert absolute control over our decisions and behavior.

To do that, however, we must recognize and accept them as real.

In *Racism by Proxy*, essayist Johnny Townsend pushes past shame, guilt, insults, and other useless approaches to show how all of us, even white people of varying privilege, benefit from increasing equity and social justice throughout our communities.

Praise for Johnny Townsend

In *Zombies for Jesus*, "Townsend isn't writing satire, but deeply emotional and revealing portraits of people who are, with a few exceptions, quite lovable."

Kel Munger, *Sacramento News and Review*

In *Sex among the Saints,* "Townsend writes with a deadpan wit and a supple, realistic prose that's full of psychological empathy… he takes his protagonists' moral struggles seriously and invests them with real emotional resonance."

Kirkus Reviews

Let the Faggots Burn: The UpStairs Lounge Fire is "a gripping account of all the horrors that transpired that night, as well as a respectful remembrance of the victims."

Terry Firma, Patheos

"Johnny Townsend's 'Partying with St. Roch' [in the anthology *Latter-Gay Saints*] tells a beautiful, haunting tale."

Kent Brintnall, Out in Print: Queer Book Reviews

Selling the City of Enoch is "sharply intelligent… pleasingly complex… The stories are full of… doubters, but there's no vindictiveness in these pages; the characters continuously poke holes in Mormonism's more extravagant absurdities, but they take very little pleasure in doing so… Many of Townsend's stories… have a provocative edge to them, but this [book] displays a great deal of insight as well… a playful, biting and surprisingly warm collection."

Kirkus Reviews

Gayrabian Nights is "an allegorical tour de force… a hard-core emotional punch."

Gay. Guy. Reading and Friends

The Washing of Brains has "A lovely writing style, and each story [is] full of unique, engaging characters… immensely entertaining."

Rainbow Awards

In *Dead Mankind Walking*, "Townsend writes in an energetic prose that balances crankiness and humor… A rambunctious volume of short, well-crafted essays…"

Kirkus Reviews

Racism by Proxy

Johnny Townsend

Print ISBN: 979-8-9877113-3-0

Ebook ISBN: 979-8-9877113-4-7

This book is a work of fiction. Names, characters, events, and dialogue are the product of the author's imagination or are used fictitiously. Any resemblance to actual persons, living or dead, is entirely coincidental.

Printed on acid-free paper.

2023

Second Edition

Cover design by Todd Engel

Special thanks to Donna Banta
for her editorial assistance

For more of Donna's own work,
please read *Seer Stone* and *False Prophet.*

Contents

"The beauty of anti-racism is that you don't have to pretend to be free of racism to be an anti-racist. Anti-racism is the commitment to fight racism wherever you find it, including in yourself. And it's the only way forward."

Ijeoma Oluo

Introduction:
Another Book on Race by an Old, White Man

Why should you read a book about bias from an old, white man?

Unless you're white, you probably shouldn't. And even if you are, you should first be reading work by Ta-Nehisi Coates, Trevor Noah, Ibram Kendi, Bryan Stevenson, Sherman Alexie, Sandra Cisneros, and many other writers from marginalized groups.

But since it isn't their responsibility to teach white people about our biases, we need to take on some of the work, too. Writers like Robin Di Angelo and Howard Zinn are great resources, as well as books like *Everyday White People Confront Racial and Social Injustice*.

So what can *I* offer that's worth your time?

Let me take a moment to share my cultural resumé:

Born and raised in New Orleans

Spent summers and holidays with extended family in rural Mississippi

Graduated from a Baptist high school

Volunteered two years as a Mormon missionary in Europe

That should be enough to reveal my white, religiously and politically conservative background, but there's a bit more:

Taught ten years at a historically Black university in the Deep South

Excommunicated from the LDS Church for being gay

Wrote the first book on the Upstairs Lounge fire, an arson at a French Quarter gay bar that killed 32 people

Wrote 50 books about gay, feminist, and other "outsider" Mormons

As a former Mormon who used to do "proxy" work for the dead in various LDS temples, I understand how easy it is to convince ourselves to engage in busywork to avoid the more difficult tasks necessary to make meaningful change in the lives of the living.

I know from experience how easy it is to shrug off our role in combatting racism and other forms of bias. "*I* didn't own slaves! *I* didn't oppress anyone!"

Because I'm like you, I've had all the same resistant reactions you have. As a result, I can show you how "white dominant culture" doesn't mean "every white person."

"Mormon culture" doesn't mean "every Mormon."

"Evangelical Christian culture" doesn't mean "every evangelical Christian."

I can show you that accepting the reality of bias doesn't mean we chose to be biased or that we're "bad" people. I can show you that empathy doesn't mean giving up our personal values.

And finally, I can assure you there's no virtue signaling here. I'm not going to call anyone out for not being world-class anti-racists. You're probably already far better at it than I'll ever be. And you don't need to agree with everything I suggest. We're all learning and growing here. None of us are going to be in the same space a year from now.

I'm simply offering my own painfully slow realizations about bias. You can either take sixty years to learn on your own… or you can skip a couple of decades by reading a few of these essays and investing just a bit of effort reflecting on them now.

There's great value when someone can consolidate their journey into a single coherent narrative. Isabel Wilkerson does a great job of this in *Caste*. But I learned the lessons in *Racism by Proxy* piecemeal and there's also value to reading the insights of others in manageable portions. Most of my essays are short enough to read as daily reflections—morning, afternoon, evening, whatever works for you—or once a week as a couple or family.

Yes, my gay ex-Mormon husband and I still practice our own version of Family Home Evening each week. There's good in every culture, after all, even various iterations of white dominant culture.

So let's celebrate the good in our lives and start reducing the bad. If you're like most people, it's what we genuinely want to do anyway. Let's stop feeling guilty, embrace positive motivations instead, and finally do what we know has to be done.

Section 1: Growing Awareness of Race

Mormons Must Stop Practicing Racism by Proxy

In cases of Munchausen Syndrome by Proxy, someone deliberately sickens another person, usually their child, because they receive so much attention and support for having a chronically ill loved one. Often, other family members and friends are shocked to discover the deception. "You couldn't have asked for a more devoted mother."

Despite extensive racist policies and doctrine throughout Mormon history, most Mormons today practice racism by proxy. "*I* didn't say that. Joseph Fielding Smith said it. Ezra Taft Benson said it. Spencer W. Kimball said it." We don't actively seek to oppress anymore. We just don't do much to stop the racist acts of others.

Another word for "proxy" could be "accessory."

In an authoritarian religion with rules so strict that drinking a cup of coffee can keep us from attending our child's wedding, we've been trained our entire lives to believe in the harshest punishment possible for the most meager of crimes. This religious mindset keeps us from understanding the damage that far harsher secular policing inflicts. We defend a police system whose primary function from the start was to oppress blacks, immigrants, and the poor.

While some police abuse may be the result of racism or a lack of training, another phenomenon could also be at work. Perhaps some officers need to feel they're "defending their community" so badly that they are pushed subconsciously to create situations that lead to the deaths of marginalized people. A kind of "Hero by Proxy."

Research suggests that people in powerful positions often lose the ability to empathize. It's called "Hubris Syndrome," and differences in brain activity can be measured. It seems likely that the compulsive need for the wealthiest people in the world to accumulate still more wealth is similarly triggered, perhaps becoming a genuine addiction.

If history is written by the winners, police reports are written by the survivors.

Anthropologist Margaret Mead was once asked what constituted the first sign of civilization 15,000 years ago. Was it a cooking pot? Arrows? Other tools of some kind?

No. The first evidence of human civilization, she said, was a broken but healed femur. Without modern medicine, such a fracture would take roughly six weeks to heal.

In the wild, animals with a broken leg don't survive. They quickly become a meal for predators. But this human had been rescued, cared for, sheltered, and fed until his leg had healed.

A 15,000-year-old healed femur, then, was the first evidence, not of human fossils, and not of human intelligence, but of "civilization."

Some of us are nurses and phlebotomists and physicians. Some of us are teachers and farmers.

Some of us are hunters and warriors.

And some of us are proxy healers or proxy predators.

When unarmed citizens, often people of color, are killed during encounters with the police, officers tell us "he tripped and fell" or "he was resisting" or "he had something in his hand." What we increasingly see, however, are officers killing unarmed suspects who weren't posing any serious threat. When we discover over and over that the cries of "Wolf!" are lies, how are we ever to know when the cry is in response to a real threat?

If it's a sin to lie, is it a sin to lie by proxy? To only and always support the claims of one side over another?

Officers must understand that being repeatedly caught lying isn't building public trust. And when 57 officers resign in protest over the suspension of two fellow officers filmed attacking an unarmed man and then lying about it, those "good" officers are telling us loud and clear the "one bad apple" defense is itself another cry of "Wolf!"

Time and again, I hear my Mormon family and friends say things like, "Well, we don't know all the details, but the guy they were trying to arrest was obviously a bad guy. He had a record. He was shoplifting. So I'm going to believe the police over that scumbag."

There's a reason serial killers often prey on prostitutes and runaways. If the Green River Killer had been murdering socialites, would the public have accepted the deaths of 49 young women without pressing for additional investigation? "It's sad what happened to those women, but they really brought it on themselves."

Despite the almost cult-like defense of cops who commit extrajudicial killings, not every police officer is "bad." But that hardly means there's no need for drastic change in our system of law enforcement.

How much more time do we spend at church teaching our kids about the dangers of bare shoulders than about either the moral or mortal consequences of racism?

I've heard family and (former) friends say, "Maybe the officer was a little too aggressive, but really, we're better off without all those criminals anyway."

Superiority by Proxy?

Honor, duty, courage, and solidarity are empty words when they're used to defend both abuse and the many lies to cover up that abuse. We cannot allow lofty principles to be used to defend the lowest behavior possible. As Mormons—really, as human beings—we're morally obligated to insist that city councils, governors, state legislatures, and Congress take immediate steps to stop the epidemic of police aggression destroying lives and communities across this nation.

If there's one thing Mormons understand, it's proxy work. But if we are to defeat racism in our churches and in our communities, it's going to take personal, active engagement. So let's put our shoulder to the wheel and get started.

Before Things Turned Violent

I didn't want to go to the protest. Demonstrations in other cities the previous two evenings had grown violent. I couldn't even chop up an onion for dinner without wearing swim goggles. How would I get through being tear gassed? And this was Seattle, where a handful of anarchists had turned a peaceful protest at the WTO conference in 1999 into the Battle of Seattle. I'd moved here after that, but friends recounted coming home from work that evening and being beaten by police officers as they stepped off the bus, unaware till that moment that chaos reigned across half the city.

One of my favorite Osmond songs growing up was "One Bad Apple Don't Spoil the Whole Bunch, Girl," and maybe that was true. But it didn't take many more than that to ruin a protest.

It was 55 degrees this afternoon and raining lightly, the kind of weather that could calm a tense mood. "Please, please, please, God," I wanted to pray, "don't let agitators and accelerationists ruin everything." Too many white people across the country were looking for a reason to dismiss the protests. I could already see friends of mine online, liberals as well as conservatives, looking for an excuse not to care.

Gary and I parked on First Avenue near Pioneer Square at the southern end of downtown, a beautiful area but a little scary in the best of times. My husband was volunteering as security for his group of socialist friends, so we'd arrived forty minutes before the protest was to begin at 3:00. He headed off to walk the last fourteen blocks to Westlake while I stayed in the truck. A temporary assignment I'd been given through one of my part-time jobs had required me to remain on my feet the entire shift three days a week and I'd developed plantar fasciitis. I didn't want to aggravate the condition any more than necessary.

I'd lost my other part-time job when the pandemic started.

I was one of the lucky ones. My loss wasn't even part of the 40 million unemployment applications of the past two months.

Watching Gary walk off, I also saw homeless people who predated the financial crisis huddled in doorway after doorway. Every store was closed. Since no one needed to pass through those doors anymore, folks practiced social distancing as best they could.

A young man across the street leaned against a building, drinking from a cup as he watched me for the next five minutes. And the next ten after that. He was *loitering.* As I was. But was he waiting for me to leave so he could vandalize the truck? Thieves had broken into Gary's pickup at least three times in the thirteen years we'd been together.

It was time now for me to head to Westlake. I secured my face mask and started walking. A block up the street, I casually glanced back to see if anyone had approached the truck. No one had, so I continued on. Some homeless folks had set up tents where they could. A dozen men and women wrapped in sleeping bags and filthy jackets huddled under the glass pergola near the totem pole in front of the closed Underground Seattle, trying to stay dry.

"Please, God, help this protest be a force for good."

Seattle officials routinely ordered sweeps of the many homeless encampments throughout the city. Tents and all other belongings were confiscated and thrown away, as if that would somehow force the destitute to change their lives for the better.

I passed another man in a sleeping bag right in the middle of the sidewalk, one hand grasping the base of his roller suitcase as he slept.

Brian, one of my liberal friends, hated these strangers. "They're breaking the law!"

It's difficult not to break the law, of course, when poverty is criminalized.

But I was scared of "them," too. As I approached a mentally ill woman shouting obscenities at the universe, I debated on how best to pass without enraging her even further. Walking too closely would certainly set her off but creating too large a safety zone by walking in the middle of the street could easily be offensive and set her off as well.

I walked along the curb, avoiding eye contact. Not seeing her was offensive, too, of course. I wished I knew the right thing to do.

Passing a narrow alley, I got a whiff of ammonia, making me aware I was already starting to feel pressure in my bladder. I'd tried not to drink much after noon today, but my diabetes made it difficult to go more than two or three hours without a pee break. We'd left the house at 1:45, yet here it was not quite 3:00, and my bladder was already demanding attention.

More and more people were heading north now, most of them white, several carrying signs. "We stand with our black brothers and sisters." "Injustice anywhere is a threat to justice everywhere." "Remaining neutral in the face of injustice is to choose the side of the oppressor."

Back in middle school, a kid in my history class had bullied me repeatedly. When I told my mother, she urged me to hit him as hard as I could. But I didn't want to. It wasn't that I was afraid he'd hit me back even harder, though that was certainly a consideration. I simply didn't want to hurt anybody at all.

But I did say something snarky to the guy, and I remembered his eyes turning cold. "I'll see you out on the playground at lunch."

During lunch period, I remained in the hallway, avoiding both the cafeteria and the playground. But a teacher discovered me and, even after I explained the situation, ordered me out of the building. I could see the disgust in her eyes because I was afraid to face the bully.

The bully, naturally, spotted me within seconds and came over to start pushing me about. I think he may have hit me in the arm as well. But what I remember most from the confrontation was the older brother of a friend of mine walking over and telling the bully to leave me alone.

The bully walked away.

All these years later, I still preferred words to physical confrontation. But I didn't have to work today and so had an opportunity to be present. Since I qualified as high risk, I'd had to opt for teleworking until my foot healed and I could return to a more normal assignment. Even now, favoring my left foot as much as possible, I could already feel the twinges that indicated possible new damage if I wasn't careful.

But I could hardly compare the risk of a small tear in a tendon to the danger blacks faced every time they stepped out of the house. I'd seen a Facebook post earlier from a man who said he never took a stroll around his mostly white neighborhood without walking his dog at the same time and asking his young daughter to accompany them. It was the only way he felt he could avoid being viewed as a criminal.

As a gay man, I understood the importance of allies. I might not be a *great* ally for Black Lives Matter, but I couldn't pretend I bore no obligation to help. The fact that I actually had a choice about participating today only proved my privilege once again.

I passed more and more police cars, officers in bulletproof vests on their bicycles, two EMT vehicles parked in anticipation. Dozens of people hurried past me on their way to Westlake. I walked slowly and carefully. Even the slight incline was making me puff.

Damn, this COVID mask was *hot*. I could barely—

Hundreds of people packed the plaza in front of Westlake. I could hear the deep voice of a speaker, but the sound system seemed faulty. Though the words were loud enough, they were too muffled to understand. The protest signs, however, declared the message most of us were feeling. "We need an elected review board!" "Demilitarize the police!" "Silence is betrayal!"

I remembered the "Silence = Death" protest signs during the height of the AIDS crisis.

Two young white women in make-up that disguised their faces stopped me on the sidewalk. "Make sure you keep your mask on. They're using tear gas over there." One of the women pointed vaguely in the direction of the plaza.

No one was yelling. Protesters weren't running in fear. I saw no smoke, smelled nothing odd. Were these women just trying to keep people from joining the main crowd?

There were hundreds more people on the sidewalk near me and on the street separating us from the thickest part of the protest. Close enough for white complacency. I backed up against a storefront and tried to gauge the mood of those around me.

Everything seemed calm. This was already the second protest of the day, and nothing untoward had occurred during the first one as far as I knew. Thank God for Seattle rain.

"We can't sit in silence," one sign floating past me along the sidewalk declared. "Arrest complicit cops!" read another. "White people—show your work!" At least half of the people here were white.

How many, I wondered, were white supremacists? Gary had attended several counterprotests at Proud Boys rallies the past few years, always volunteering as security for his friends. The Pacific Northwest, I'd found to my dismay, was home to more than one white supremacist group. Patriot Prayer had headquarters up here. A group of Three Percenters was in the area, too. I'd moved away from the South fifteen years ago, for God's sake. Things were supposed to be better here.

I couldn't see Gary anywhere in the crowd. If things got ugly…

I heard a rushing sound increasing in intensity. OMG, what was happening? Was that noise from gas cannisters going off? I looked around quickly.

The crowd across the street was cheering something the speaker had just said.

Stop being such a scaredy-cat.

It was only 3:20, and I really had to pee. But another surprise like that and I wouldn't need to worry about trying to find a bathroom.

The two white women near me kept stopping newcomers and warning them about the tear gas.

There was no tear gas.

Forty feet to my right, a black woman began yelling loudly at a white man. Everyone around them watched the altercation in silence. Finally, I heard the woman say, "We don't need any of you goddamn anarchists here! Get out!" After another minute of her outburst, the white man, clad all in black, walked off.

People turned their attention back to the speaker, clapping every once in a while. Apparently, others could make out the words I couldn't.

But did anyone believe that anarchist had simply gone home in defeat? And how many others were out there? Some days, I absolutely loathed people.

Some days, even myself.

A white man sitting on the sidewalk beside me handed out juice packets to homeless people who wandered by. Maybe they weren't even wandering. They seemed to know him, went right up to him. Maybe he did this all the time.

Another white man, barefaced, marched up to me in disgust. "Why are you wearing a mask? The pandemic's a hoax!" He walked away, shouting at other stupid people in the crowd. Most of us wore cloth masks, some wore paper masks, and a couple wore some version of gas mask. One man walked about in a snorkeling mask over his N95.

I patted my jacket pocket to make sure my swim goggles were ready if the warning from the two white women eventually turned out to be true.

Only 3:30, and Gary had told me the protest would probably last two hours. If I walked back to Pioneer Square, perhaps I could pee in an alley.

A black man walked by, holding his sign up high. "I can't breathe!" Several of his friends followed behind as he moved on, each with a sign of his own.

"Listen!"

"Don't shoot! I'm asleep!"

"I can't believe we're still protesting this shit!"

Seattleites were all about recycling. I'd seen that last sign at another protest three or four years ago.

Three medics in PPE walked by with their gear, heading deeper into the crowd. Had something happened? Everyone still seemed calm.

A black woman in her late thirties moved up to an empty spot along the wall beside me. Her sign read, "PTSD—Present Traumatic Stress Disorder."

What the hell was wrong with so many white people? If a neighbor moved in next door and came over to let us know our dog had gotten out of the back yard, sharing also that her three-year-old had been mauled by a dog a few months earlier, we wouldn't tell her to "Get over it already" while turning up our nose in disgust. We wouldn't say, "Well, *my* dog didn't hurt your kid!" We'd try to be decent neighbors.

Wouldn't we?

While perhaps 85% of the crowd at Westlake today was divided fairly equally between blacks and whites, a smaller but significant portion was composed of Asians and Latinx, with a few Native Americans and a smattering of other groups as well.

A gay Argentinian friend of mine hated the term "Latinx," pointing out it was nearly unpronounceable in Spanish.

Damn, I needed to pee.

But I needed to stay at least till 4:00. A protest wasn't a place to just check in, say you were there, and head back out, marking off a box to prove you were "good." I needed to study more on how to be a better ally. Almost every form of oppression on the planet, after all, was tied either to racism or sexism.

Four young black men gathered along the wall several feet away, leaning in to talk like football players in a huddle. I was getting a bad vibe. They seemed suspicious.

Unless that was my subconscious bias popping up yet again.

This was all so hard. Not as hard as walking home with Skittles, of course, but still challenging. Was that why people wanted to wash their hands of it?

A young white man joined the two white women on my other side. The guy hooked something black to his belt. It was the shape of a soda can, but only half the length, and black. Was that a flash grenade? Or were they called flash bombs? Flash bangs?

With the growing political unrest in this country, it was clear I needed to learn some new words.

For now, I was going to use my diabetes as an excuse and start looking for a bathroom. Perhaps a Starbucks might be open farther from the demonstration. At about 3:50, I started heading south. Two blocks later, I glanced to my left and saw a huge crowd up on Fifth marching toward City Hall or King County jail. Or maybe police headquarters. The three buildings were all within a couple of blocks of each other.

Every store I passed was closed, even Starbucks. Several store owners had boarded up their windows. For all I knew, that had happened weeks ago when the city was first put under a stay-at-home order. This was the first time in two and a half months that I'd ventured more than a few blocks from home.

It was impossible to know how much of the tension in protests across the country this week was a result of the relentless police killings of unarmed blacks, how much was a product of the non-stop barrage of hateful rhetoric coming from the White House, and how much was simply a consequence of forced isolation coupled with increasing economic despair.

That morning, a good friend of mine had posted on FB her disgust with the riots. "Listen up, black people! This does nothing for your cause." And with that, she brushed off the need to care any longer about solving the root problems. If those bad, stupid black people were going to behave like animals, white people didn't need to concern themselves over something as minor as racism. Criminals got what they deserved.

I remembered my dad, a High Priest in our Mormon congregation, buying a CB radio back in the 1970s, so happy for its help in avoiding cops when we drove two hours to visit his parents in Mississippi. He could finally speed with impunity.

Our home in a white suburb of New Orleans was burglarized twice by white teenagers.

I'd watched on the news yesterday evening as a peaceful, unresisting black CNN reporter and his crew were arrested while they broadcast live from Minneapolis. I watched as a white reporter in Louisville and her crew were shot with pepper balls by officers aiming directly at them.

Whose cause did that further?

I passed a homeless woman in running shorts, shivering next to a boarded up window in the rain.

I had almost reached Pioneer Square again, but I didn't want to pee on the street. Gary had asked me not to ride public transportation during the pandemic, and I had no desire to, either, but Metro had begun blocking off seats on its buses to force people to keep a reasonable distance while riding. I was tired, my left foot hurt, my bladder was about to burst, and I just wanted to go home. So when a 7 Prentice pulled up to the bus stop, I stepped aboard and found an unblocked seat.

As we passed the light rail station in the International District, I could see another huge crowd heading north toward police headquarters.

The bus had hardly gone three blocks down Rainier Avenue when a police car with its siren blaring zoomed past us heading downtown, on *our* side of the street.

That couldn't be good. But I didn't want to text Gary. If anything bad was going on over there, I didn't want to distract him.

The bus was crowded, a white homeless man with filthy pants sitting on top of a "Seat Closed" sign across the aisle, another white man who looked down and out but perhaps not homeless sat next to me and talked to a black woman a seat behind us. Someone boarded with their dog. Another man carried two bags of groceries.

Some guy kept talking and talking and talking, apparently to no one. A few minutes later, I heard a black man address the talker. "We're gonna give you a pass because you're crazy," he said.

My phone rang, and I saw Gary's name on the screen. "Where are you?" he asked. I could barely hear him.

"I'm good," I told him. "I'm—"

He interrupted me with a question. I tried to hear him in all the noise around me and then he stopped talking in mid-sentence. I called him back, but there was no answer.

Fuck! If he was in trouble, I couldn't help him by calling.

Was this the day neo-Nazis finally showed up with an assault weapon and mowed down thirty people? They'd been caught trying to blow up a gay bar on Capitol Hill several years earlier. And I knew the Boogaloo movement wanted to foment another civil war. In a world where the President of the United States could retweet, "The only good Democrat is a dead Democrat," anything was possible.

I clenched for several seconds to calm my bladder.

Finally, we reached my stop near the end of the line. I pulled the cord, the only thing I'd touched while aboard the bus. After we pulled to a stop, I stood up, avoiding the support bars, and headed to the door. I passed a black man asleep next to his belongings and stepped off.

The rain was pouring now. Thank God. Surely, that would slow down whatever was happening downtown.

I reached the house five minutes later, just a few minutes past 5:00. As soon as I unlocked the door, my phone vibrated and sent out a screech. "Emergency Alert!" The mayor had issued a curfew, effective at 5:00.

I ran to the bathroom and let out a long stream.

Remembering the hundreds of homeless people I'd seen that day who couldn't even use the bathroom in the public library anymore.

When I turned on the TV a moment later, I gasped. Cars were on fire downtown. Smoke from the promised tear gas was everywhere. A white man who might have grabbed a rifle from a vandalized police vehicle had the weapon ripped out of his hand by a white officer. People were breaking windows at Nordstrom and other stores, running inside and handing goods to people on the sidewalk.

Every one of the looters looked black.

Goddammit.

I'd seen a meme on FB earlier. "Looting isn't protesting. But murder isn't policing." Yet I knew almost all of my friends and family, both Republican and Democrat, were only going to remember the looting, not the murder of George Floyd or Breonna Taylor or anyone else. I knew my friends were also going to quibble over the term "murder" but would have no trouble lumping everyone at the protests with "thugs."

They'd already been saying for days that we shouldn't judge all cops by the bad behavior of a few bad officers. But they were already judging the entire Black Lives Matter movement by the actions of a minority of blacks destroying property.

On the TV in front of me, one of the news cameras zeroed in on several of the looters in the store, and I realized to my surprise that over half of them were white. They were wearing ski masks covering everything but their eyes and mouths. Black ski masks. But at least half of those looters were white. Not all of them. There were clearly some blacks looting as well.

And I knew most people across the country would only see black people committing crimes. The only time they bothered to notice black people at all.

And the looting and attacks on police cars might well have taken place without any prodding by white provocateurs. There was plenty of well-earned anger out there.

A reporter onscreen lamented that the protest had been going so well "before things turned violent." Did he *still* not understand the violence perpetrated against blacks for centuries?

I wondered if the black protesters I'd seen today wished I hadn't come down to Westlake at all. Had they been glad to see so many white faces, feeling they'd finally gained allies who'd stand with them when it counted, or had experience warned them to expect a hijacking?

Agents had infiltrated protests and strikes for the past 150 years, when women demanded suffrage, when blacks demanded suffrage, when workers demanded fair wages and safe working conditions. It was *always* going to happen, especially when the stakes were high.

But women did have the right to vote now. So did blacks. Workers did have unions.

So maybe as a society we'd finally make progress on this front, too, despite the sabotage.

The truth is we would never be able to sift out who did what at every protest and what group they were part of. The best we could do was keep the focus on the source of the actual problem—structural racism that led inevitably to individual racist atrocities.

I'd texted Gary the moment I turned on the television to let him know I'd made it home safely. He hadn't responded, hadn't answered when I called one more time. I kept my phone in front of me, glancing at it every fifteen seconds as if it were a rearview mirror.

Gary was a smart guy. He'd be home soon.

I remembered the twelve people huddled under the pergola in Pioneer Square.

The phone rang. Gary had made it back to the truck with two elderly women from his political group. I assured him I was fine, he assured me they were as well, and he told me he'd be home as soon as he could drop them off at their place. "But, man, I really gotta pee."

I was waiting on the front porch when he drove up in the rain, holding the front door open as he ran past me to the bathroom.

Privilege Doesn't Mean Life Is Perfect

As soon as folks like me hear the words "white privilege," we often experience a knee-jerk reaction. We're about to be attacked, and we immediately gear up for a counterattack.

"I'm *poor*! I have an eating disorder! My parents beat me! I never had a chance to go to college!"

So let's talk instead about other types of privilege.

Have you ever hurt your finger or wrist and been forced temporarily to use your other hand to perform a simple task?

It wasn't until I tried to cut a sheet of paper with scissors using my left hand that I realized the word "scissors" was actually a shortened version of the correct term, "right-handed scissors."

But why are "left-handed scissors" *called* "left-handed scissors" while "right-handed scissors" are given the more generic "scissors"?

I was in college before I saw a left-handed desk for the first time. It baffled me why anyone would design a desk so poorly. Even then, it didn't occur to me that left-handed people needed such a design until someone pointed it out.

And it wasn't until I noticed a left-handed classmate writing, her hand moving directly over the fresh ink and smudging it, that I recognized even such a simple act could be a legitimate challenge.

Privilege is not having to think about something because it's just never been an issue.

That's all privilege is. It doesn't mean life is never hard for any right-handed person. Such a claim would be preposterous. It just means that right-handedness isn't one of the things making life difficult.

I'm also able-bodied. I never thought about what it means to have two functioning legs and two functioning arms until I dated a man born with only one arm. Several months after we began seeing each other, I tried to spend an entire day using only one arm, to get a glimpse into the life of a man I thought I knew well.

It was *hard.* Manageable, perhaps, if you could cheat once or twice an hour, just for a few seconds each time.

Of course, if you really only have one arm, you can't cheat.

Fortunately, after my boyfriend and I broke up a year or so later, I was quickly able to forget my able-bodied privilege. It became "the norm" again.

Does being able-bodied mean I've been blissfully free of difficulties throughout my life?

Of course not. But being able-bodied is not one of them.

Clearly, however, that doesn't mean being able-bodied isn't a *tremendous* privilege making life inordinately easier for me than it is for those who aren't. Still, we aren't morally deficient because we're able bodied. It's not a sin. We don't have to apologize for it.

But it's *also* not a sin to insist on ADA access allowing others with mobility issues to use the same buildings we do. It's not morally deficient to add captions or sub-titles to video presentations.

So… what other privileges do I enjoy? Well, I'm a good speller. Never made it to a national competition, but I did place second in a parish spelling bee.

Whoo hoo!

(Yes, that's the way you spell it. Though it's also spelled woohoo, woo hoo, and whoo-hoo.)

Hoo boy.

As an adult, I was surprised to discover that spelling isn't strongly correlated with intelligence. Some intelligent people are good spellers and some aren't. Some less intelligent people are good at spelling and some aren't. Spelling ability isn't even particularly well correlated with education.

I didn't earn my ability to spell, but I do enjoy the privilege it affords, including the belief employers often have that I'm more intelligent than others. I guarantee you I don't go out of my way to explain in job interviews that I'm not as smart as I look on paper. If I get hired, my supervisor will figure it out soon enough. In the meantime, I use the privilege to edge out the competition.

I grew up in the Deep South. That means I've been eating boiled peanuts since childhood. I like roasted peanuts, too. And what kid doesn't love peanut butter?

I'm not responsible for the privilege of not experiencing anaphylaxis and dying when a misguided teacher insists I stop being picky and eat the snack provided.

It's also a privilege not being allergic to penicillin or pet dander. It's a privilege not to have been born with a cleft palate. It's a privilege to drink milk without subsequently farting as much as a cow.

Having an "innie" belly button isn't any better than having an "outie" except we've artificially created a stigma around outies.

I stop when I see a red light, even if it's one of those horizontal ones instead of the vertical kind I'm used to. Because I can recognize red and understand the meaning we've artificially linked to that color.

I'm privileged to have "normal" skin rather than chronic psoriasis.

It's even a privilege to have pain receptors. Have you seen the horrific lives children without them often lead?

I don't walk around every day conscious of these biological traits. That's privilege.

When I sang in the New Orleans Gay Men's Chorus, one of the other chorus members had perfect pitch. He couldn't understand why everyone else was unable to perform at his level.

As a Mormon missionary in Italy, I couldn't understand why some of my fellow missionaries had so much difficulty learning Italian. It was an easy language. I even did well studying Russian and Hebrew, though Hebrew was challenging because it was written right to left.

Should we feel guilty if we have perfect pitch? Are we bad for being right-handed? Am I terrible because learning languages comes easily to me?

Being privileged for any quality or talent or biological fact does not mean we've done something wrong. White people need to stop feeling defensive when someone points out our privilege. It may sound like an accusation, but it's simply a statement of fact. We *are* privileged. Our society favors us. We may never have deliberately done anything to earn the favor or to create disfavor toward others, but we do benefit from the privilege that exists.

It's OK to say so.

Would you be ashamed to state that water is wet?

And it doesn't mean everything else in our life has gone beautifully. Someone with white skin can also be hearing impaired. He or she might be transgender or allergic to nuts or dyslexic or have any number of other challenges.

Some people have an eidetic memory. Imagine what kind of difficulties most of us would face if society was shaped assuming *everyone* had an eidetic memory.

Some people are able to smell things the rest of us can't. They can smell Parkinson's disease in people years before any medical tests can diagnose it. Some can smell cancer.

What would life be like if the only way to successfully navigate the world was to be able to detect diseases by smell months or years before science could diagnose them?

Just because the privilege white people in Western culture enjoy is more common and more normalized doesn't make it any less arbitrary.

I expect part of the resistance we feel to being told we're privileged is because we've only recently had to start thinking about being white.

We don't like thinking about it because we unnecessarily tie it to guilt.

I don't feel guilty that I can hear music. I listen to music and enjoy it.

After a terrible disaster, sometimes the survivors feel survivor's guilt. Why did we survive when others just as deserving didn't? Perhaps we tell ourselves we survived because we were a little smarter, tried harder to escape. But we're all too aware many smart people who tried extremely hard did not escape.

Some survivors are never able to enjoy life again. It doesn't feel fair to allow themselves happiness others can't experience.

But such guilt serves no one. Much better to enjoy the privilege of being alive, while at the same time working to make sure whatever caused the disaster doesn't happen to other people.

The only behavior tied to privilege that can be considered a fault is feeling so defensive that we refuse to treat others equally, whatever the color of their skin, or their ability to sing, or their religion, or their ability to walk, or anything else.

When I hear my white friends and family yelling, "I worked hard for what I have! My life's been just as difficult as anyone's! How *dare* you say I'm privileged!" I realize they feel robbed of their suffering, robbed of their triumphs, robbed of their character.

It's a misunderstanding of the term.

We're not bad for using right-handed scissors.

We're not bad for taking a walk around the block.

We're not bad for admiring a beautiful painting.

We might very well be bad, though, if we don't bother making reasonable accommodations for folks lacking our privileges, to provide equitable access to all the things *we* have access to, whether that's a building, a college education, a job, or anything else.

But there's no need to make these improvements out of guilt. We can make the changes because we want others to enjoy life a little more.

While we're at it, we can make our own privileged lives easier, too, by guaranteeing tuition-free college and vocational training to all, and universal healthcare, and a living wage. Equity is good for able-bodied white folks who eat peanuts, too.

It will be an amazing privilege to live in an equitable society.

Choosing *not* to develop empathy, though, and not acknowledge reality, isn't much of a privilege for anyone at all.

Protesting at a Black Lives Matter Rally Revealed More of My Biases

One of the most discouraging lessons for me as I try to become anti-racist rather than merely "non-racist" is the near constant discovery of the many biases I still harbor. Last Sunday, protesters held a Black Lives Matter rally in my Rainier Beach neighborhood, and my husband decided to meet with some elderly white friends at the start of the protest on Othello. I wasn't up for walking the entire route from there to the Safeway just down the hill from me, so I told Gary I'd meet him at the end of the march. I'd injected extra insulin both the night before and again in the morning to decrease the chance I'd need to urinate before the rally was over. The march was supposed to begin at 2:00, and I started down the hill around 2:20, knowing even my abbreviated walk would take me twenty-five minutes. I expected to find a nice, safe place to observe everything in plenty of time.

Walking down the last part of 51st, I passed a house with a dozen balloons staked in the front yard. A young man who'd just graduated high school had been shot in his car and killed a few weeks earlier, around 10:30 at night. I remembered that upon first hearing of the shooting, my immediate thought had been that the young football player about to begin his studies at the University of Washington was probably black.

You know, black teen violence and all.

Nope. He was white, I learned. And seeing the balloons reminded me that I still made biased assumptions all the time.

Finally on Rainier, I saw food booths, voter registration booths, and music speakers set up in a cordoned off part of the Safeway parking lot, the section where two young men had been shot and killed a couple of days after the football player. Our local news reports had described the shooting as "gang related." Was that a code word for black, I wondered? Were these Asian gang members? Latino? White gangs? The area where the rally had started on Othello was considered the most diverse zip code west of the Mississippi River, and my neighborhood couldn't be far behind. Why should "gang" necessarily mean "black"?

Except in our heads.

When I'd first read *Le Morte d'Arthur* in grad school, I'd been struck that the Knights of the Round Table were nothing more than a violent gang, complete with gang colors. When they encountered knights wearing any other color, they fought, sometimes to the death, even if there was no provocation. It was all about "courage" and "honor."

When police officers stood up for each other no matter what, were they the Jets or the Sharks?

Several protesters walked around with signs, and by the time I reached Henderson, I could see a group of about twenty-five folks chanting on the corner. Already, I'd seen a wide variety of people. There were black protesters, white, Asian, Latinx, some old but mostly young. A good many protesters wheeled their young children in strollers. A few carried infants. Eight-year-olds waved signs.

I didn't have a sign. The art supply store where I usually bought poster board for protests was closed because of the pandemic, and the one sign I had on hand at home read, "What have you got against a stable climate?"

Metaphorically, the slogan was still appropriate, since a healthy and stable social atmosphere benefitted everyone.

"Demand Seattle PD Accountability!"

"86 Shots. Why?"

"Breathing is a right!"

Cars passing the corner honked in support. A dump truck driver blasted what sounded like a foghorn long and loud. Drivers raised their fists out car windows or sunroofs in solidarity. One was a middle-aged Asian woman. Several young Asians were in the group of two dozen protesters on the corner. One held a sign saying, "Chinese and Lao Black Lives Matter." I couldn't tell from this distance if the word "for" had been inserted before "Black," and the odd grammar confused me.

Until I remembered that interracial relationships weren't limited to white and black or white and Asian. Even at a Black Lives Matter rally, I kept thinking in white-centric terms.

Two police motorcycles pulled out into the intersection unexpectedly, causing two cars to screech to a stop. The officers stood beside their bikes and indicated that the northbound lanes of Rainier were now closed to traffic. That must mean the marchers were on their way.

The protesters on the corner began chanting, "Blue Lives Matter! Black Lives Matter!" in a round, half of them calling out the first chant and the others the second chant. "Blue Lives Matter!" "Black Lives Matter!" "Blue Lives Matter!" "Black Lives Matter!"

How nice, I thought. This was going to be a peaceful protest. Some of the worst violence had occurred over a week earlier at a demonstration downtown—Gary and I had left just before it erupted—and since then, only the protests up on Capitol Hill still got rough late in the evening.

Glued to the national news every night, we'd watched as an elderly man with a cane shuffled along a Salt Lake City street until police officers knocked him down for moving too slowly, as police in North Carolina vandalized a first aid table set up by nurses. We'd watched as police vehicles plowed into crowds, as officers slashed tires on cars they assumed belonged to protesters. We'd watched as they pulled down face masks and zapped non-violent protesters with pepper spray. We'd watched as a woman pleaded with officers not to take her insulin. We'd watched as hundreds of reporters all across the country were arrested, were beaten with clubs and shields, as they were shot with pepper balls, with rubber bullets that left one reporter permanently blinded in one eye.

A few more people began arriving from the neighborhood, others who apparently also wanted to avoid the march down Rainier and just be present for the conclusion. A young black man joined a friend, telling him he'd just gotten off work. Several young women in hijabs held signs. An elderly woman in a brilliant yellow khimar limped by and joined a few other protesters. Rainier Beach was home to several thousand African immigrants.

Probably half the protesters I'd seen so far were black, the others a mixture of everything else. Almost everyone wore face masks to help guard against COVID-19.

A black man waving an American flag drove by.

Most of the signs were in English, some in Spanish, some in unidentifiable languages using the Latin alphabet but others using Asian characters, hanzi or kanji or something else. I was woefully ignorant. At least the "Filipinos for Black Lives Matter!" was clear enough.

The protesters on the corner were chanting again. "Get your knee off my neck!"

After two or three minutes of that, the chant turned into, "No justice! No peace! Prosecute the Police!" for the next few minutes.

It was only 3:30, and I was already tired. My plantar fasciitis was almost healed, but my feet were feeling the stress from standing so long. The weight I'd gained during the stay-at-home order was putting additional strain on my lower back. I was mortified every time I looked in the bathroom mirror, knowing everyone judged me the instant they saw me. Most of my adult life, I'd been thin and made friends easily, but now as a fat man, I was aware how much effort it took for people to hide their disgust at my appearance. I couldn't stop judging myself as well.

Earlier that morning, I'd read an essay by a trans man comparing how he'd been treated as a woman to how he was treated now as a man.

Hadn't *Black Like Me* been published in 1961? The book was as old as I was, and there were still folks in positions of power calling for a military crackdown on non-violent protesters doing no more than demanding the right to life.

I sat down at the bus stop near the corner, but only a couple of minutes later, a black man in his forties hobbled up with his suitcase and I moved off so he could sit. I headed over to the bus stop on the opposite side of the street but could only rest for ten minutes there before another homeless man came over to ask for a light.

I looked at my watch. Going to protests was sure boring. I'd heard some of my friends claim the "riots"—the word they preferred—were all about people being stuck at home too long and just needing something to do. But protests weren't fun. They weren't thrilling and exciting. The forecast today was for rain, so I'd worn my jacket, which also made it easier to carry my cell phone and the swim goggles I might need if the police fired chemical weapons. But the sky was sunny and hot.

And the marchers were nowhere in sight.

Some of these tedious protests lasted several hours. Even during my ACT UP days in the 1980s, I hadn't been able to last more than an hour or two at a protest.

I thought of Charles, a man I'd met at a French Quarter gay bar. He was from Shreveport, but we met in his hotel on Dauphine for all of our subsequent hook ups. He liked to give me hickeys and spit in my face during sex. Totally not my thing, but I liked knowing he was having fun.

It was a story I couldn't even tell my gay friends. "It's people like that who give gays a bad name."

Charles led the first ACT UP protest I participated in at City Hall. I remembered him pulling a noose around his neck as the news team filmed.

He was dead a year later.

"Blue Lives Matter!" "Black Lives Matter!" The group on the corner was chanting again. I was a little closer now, and something seemed off about the chant. It almost sounded like they were adding an unnecessary -s. "Blues Lives Matter!" Odd.

I thought about John Belushi. But the chant must be referencing blues singers in the African American community.

I tried listening more carefully. Were they saying, "Jews Lives Matter!"? A sizeable Jewish community lived in Seward Park not too far away.

Oh my god.

They were saying, "Whose Lives Matter? Black Lives Matter!" How could I be so fucking stupid?

By 4:00, the leading edge of the march was approaching. More and more people were arriving from the neighborhood as well. A young black woman walked past wearing a shirt that said "Selma." Another's shirt said simply, "Melanin."

A white woman held a sign up high. "Racism is small dick energy."

Others walked by with still more signs. "No new youth jail!"

"Support black businesses!"

"It's time to use our outside voices!"

With that, I heard more chanting. "Hands up! Guns down!" followed by, "The people united will never be defeated!" An oldie but a goodie.

A young woman rolled by in a wheelchair. Another woman set up a table to sell COVID masks sewn with African prints.

And now hordes of people passed along Rainier toward the Safeway. I walked ahead, not wanting to be caught in the thick of the crowd. I'd stumbled once on Bourbon Street during Mardi Gras and been carried along by a throng of revelers, my feet not even touching the ground for several seconds. Ever since, I'd had a fear of being trampled.

I'd seen on the news earlier a police officer on horseback in some other city deliberately trampling a female protester with her hands up. Who could even keep track anymore where the latest act of brutality had been committed?

As I moved ahead, looking back every few seconds to monitor the progress of the marchers, I realized I wasn't actually part of the protest, after all, despite my intentions. I was merely a spectator. As a white man, someone not even holding a sign, how could anyone know I was there in support rather than for some other reason? I could see now that most of the protesters with signs had easily found materials without heading to the art supply store. There were signs made from pizza boxes, from Amazon boxes, from whatever people had lying about the house or in their back yard.

"Justice is a choice!"

"Don't hope for change. MAKE change!"

"Stay woke!" The protester could probably have added a second phrase, "They shoot you when you're asleep."

Two black men and a black woman sat on horses on the corner of 51st and Rainier. One held up a Black Lives Matter flag. Another held the red, black, and green striped Pan-African flag. Each rider held a fist high in the air. Several protesters posed with the horses and their riders. It looked inspiring… until I saw two white women stand beside the horses, smiling broadly for their photos.

It made me question if the women were treating these other protesters as props, the photos evidence of their white goodness. I knew I'd be writing about the afternoon's events later. Did that mean I was doing the same thing with words, using the entire rally as a prop?

A protester walked by with a sign proclaiming, "White silence is violence." Another sign explained, "We just want to live." Still another sign declared, "Love your black neighbor as yourself."

Love even in a committed relationship was complicated. I hadn't seen Gary in the crowd yet, wondered if he was disappointed I hadn't walked the full route with him, if he'd been disappointed I hadn't joined him in the protest he'd participated in a few days earlier. He regularly took part in more protests than I did.

Someone walked by with a Rainbow flag, traditionally used for LGBTQ pride. This one had two additional stripes, one brown and one black.

I already knew two gay friends who didn't approve of the change.

A young black man passed with a sign. "How many weren't filmed?"

Another young black man was on his cell. "No," he told someone firmly, "you've *got* to get down here. You *need* to be here."

A white woman held her sign high over the crowd. "All mothers were summoned when he asked for his mama."

Two signs with apple themes passed in close succession. "Good apples don't keep the bad apples around to spoil the whole bunch."

"Are you a bad apple or a good apple?"

I could hear the question as asked by Glenda, the Witch of the North.

"You can look the other way but you can never say again you did not know."

People were starting to drift off, but looking north along Rainier, I could still see hundreds of people who hadn't arrived yet. Two or three thousand must have passed me already.

I'd seen a sign on the news earlier. "Carpe momentum." Nothing like a dead language to talk about racism.

We just *had* to accomplish something meaningful *now*, at this moment. *I* had to, *Gary* had to. We *all* had to.

But I felt the same embarrassment I used to feel at church dances. If I went out on the floor and danced, I was going to look like a fool.

It was clear many more biases would keep popping up every time I tried to be an ally. I'd seen a video once: "Stupid dog tricks." I expected I could probably compile one depicting my "Stupid white mistakes."

I hadn't felt like a fool dancing with a man for the first time at a gay Mardi Gras ball.

A young black woman walked by with a sign. “Pessimism is a tool of oppression.”

I knew that people in almost every major European city, people throughout Latin America, in several African countries, in Australia and the Philippines and South Korea and Japan, were protesting along with us.

I started making my way slowly back up the hill, standing aside to let other pedestrians pass. The pandemic wasn’t over yet. Twenty-five minutes later, I reached the house. I opened the recycle bin and pulled out a piece of cardboard that had previously housed a case of vanilla protein shakes. I took it inside and started making a sign.

Train Up a Child in the Bias He Should Know

"Train up a child in the way he should go, and when he is old he will not depart from it" (Proverbs 22:6). That's as true for the biases we learn as well as for our religious worldview.

Bias is a learned, automatic reaction, either positive or negative. When I was a Mormon missionary in Italy, my companion and I rented *Fiddler on the Roof* to show local members. We wanted to help those struggling with Catholic backgrounds understand it was possible to break free of "Tradition!" The flip side was working with members whose children were no longer interested in the LDS Church.

I recently joined a Facebook group for missionaries who served under my mission president and was shocked to see that several formerly rebellious colleagues were now stalwart members. One elder had earned money for his mission by selling drugs. Another had worked as a loan shark. Serving was to fulfill family expectations. If they believed, it was only nominally. I was surprised they'd even completed their missions, much less remained in the Church for decades.

I left the Church only a few years after returning home and have also remained close to Mormonism. My former companions will say it's because "the Spirit" is trying to call me to repentance, that I can never really deny "the truth" I'd once testified of every day. But the facts are that ex-Jehovah's Witnesses feel the same ties to their past. So do ex-Catholics and ex-Sunnis and ex-Lubavitchers.

I'm 59 and have never drunk an alcoholic beverage. I've never smoked a cigarette, never taken any illicit drugs. And while I no longer believe drinking coffee is a sin, some mornings when I prepare a pot for my husband, I experience a brief, "Oh my heck, what am I doing?"

An atheist now, I still find myself wanting to pray, "in the name of Jesus Christ."

Most Mormons reading this just gasped at the word "atheist." Or frowned. Or felt pity. And your upbringing led you to experience it. Automatically.

I watch *Zoey's Extraordinary Playlist* or *Snowpiercer* or *Space Force* and realize I'm interpreting a certain line or situation through Mormon eyes. I can't hear a news report about Navajos with COVID or about missing indigenous women or contested pipelines on Native land without thinking, at least for a moment, about their "Lamanite" ancestors.

So when my Mormon friends and family tell me they resent being accused of bias against Blacks or others, I realize it's simply because they don't understand how implicit bias works. It's unconscious, part of the culture we grow up in, not something we choose. In the case of Mormons, we were taught (not very long ago) that Black people were cursed because they weren't vigilant in the Pre-Existence. "Bigfoot" was probably Cain. Prophet

Brigham Young taught that anyone involved in an interracial relationship should be executed.

Lamanites were cursed because of their wickedness. But once they repent, their skin will turn white again.

An LDS leader can't snap his fingers, say the Church doesn't teach racism anymore, and expect that to erase years of direct and subliminal messages. American Mormons are part of the national culture as well, which has also engrained biases into our subconscious. Learning what we've been taught doesn't make us bad people. The bias is inevitable. How could we *not* learn those lessons? But refusing to acknowledge bias exists, when we have so much evidence it does, *is* morally unacceptable.

If I'm still influenced decades later by my short time in the LDS Church, do we expect that just because we mean well, we're somehow immune to learning, to influence, to culture we've experienced our entire lives?

We all swear we don't pay attention to stupid commercials, but companies wouldn't spend millions of dollars influencing us if it didn't gain them hundreds of millions in return.

I only lived in Italy two years, and yet forty years after I first stepped off the plane in Rome, I can't help but turn up my nose at inauthentic Italian food. I listen to the news about growing fascism in Italy differently than those who didn't visit the ruins of Mussolini's house personally. One of the Italian missionaries I worked with was anti-Reagan. She was later anti-Bush and then anti-Bush II, yet a woman who remained committed to the Church and its conservative morals the rest of her life.

Did you just experience another knee-jerk reaction?

It's not a sin to be biased. It's inescapable. The pressing choice before us today is what to *do* about injustices caused by racial and other forms of bias.

My Mormon background still tells me that we must make amends for the harm we've caused and from here on out "Do what is right and let the consequence follow."

So let's try just a little harder to reach across artificial divisions, celebrate with one another, and "Drink, l'chaim, to life!"

Don't panic. 7-Up is perfectly acceptable.

All or Nothing Racism

"How dare you judge me! *I* never did anything to you! *My* ancestors weren't slave owners! You saying that white people are racist *is* racist!"

To reduce this emotional resistance, racial equity trainers often use the term "white dominant culture," explaining to offended whites that it doesn't refer to *all* white people. Although most members of the white dominant culture are quick to understand that *some* white people doing bad things doesn't mean all white people are bad, many of them seem unable to make this same cognitive leap when considering the actions of others.

The reality that *some* protesters are violent, that *some* participate in looting, shouldn't mean that *all* people protesting injustice are bad, or that the issue being protested isn't valid. Those who defend the police after yet another unprovoked killing rush to point out that not *all* officers are bad, that it's not fair to cast them all as racist, but the same concession is rarely offered in return.

Does the fact that this or that Republican was caught beating his spouse mean that all Republicans are abusers? Then why does the fact that this or that Democrat was caught committing insider trading mean all Democrats are white-collar looters?

Jews can be swindled by pyramid schemes run by Jews as easily as Mormons can be conned by Mormon multilevel marketers. Affinity fraud is successful because we trust others of our own “kind” without questioning. It’s in our DNA to be tribal.

A legitimate problem in our society is “Republican dominant culture.” Many individual Republicans are clearly good, well-intentioned people. But just as a “good” white person is obligated to actively work to break down structural racism, a “good” Republican must work to tear down the racist (and sexist and homophobic and xenophobic) parts of Republican culture. Not to do so is to perpetuate the oppressive behavior of others, which at best makes the “good” person an accessory to oppression. Are accessories to murder, even third-degree murder, truly eligible for the label “good”?

“Good” Democrats must stop supporting candidates and policies that oppress workers. They must stop their “unhappy acceptance” of bills that help fossil fuel corporations continue escalating the climate crisis. They must stop being accessories to the dismantling of the postal service, to the denial of healthcare to millions of Americans, to foreign policy that oppresses hundreds of millions of people all over the world.

One of my missionary companions in Naples, having a bad day, spit in the face of a teenager he found obnoxious. On another occasion, this companion threatened to break my fingers. On another, he threatened to kill me. And he was serious.

My sin? I'd witnessed him taking a dump on the side of the road when we couldn't get home in time for him to use the toilet.

But "tattling" was wrong, so problem missionaries often went unreported.

I also didn't report my zone leader who physically attacked two young gay men riding a Vespa.

Mission leader after mission leader, though, told me it was my "duty" to hound junior companions to teach more lessons.

After returning to the U.S., I was called as second counselor in the Elders' Quorum and as Single Adult rep for my ward, required to attend "leadership meetings" early Sunday mornings before the regular three-hour church schedule.

We told each other about the issues those under our leadership were experiencing, ostensibly to find solutions, though the most consistent outcome seemed to be our feelings of importance and superiority. "Poor Sister So-and-So. Let's see what we can do to help her overcome her problems."

"Poor Brother So-and-So. Can you check in on him again this week?"

I suppose we did occasionally manage to help, but mostly we just gossiped in the name of the Lord. Many of us suspected something was off, but we sincerely wanted to "do good," and our participation proved we were part of the in group of do-gooders.

Worse was when local leaders sometimes asked people to spy on those problem members. Friends in Salt Lake told me how folks were assigned to write down the license plate numbers of cars parked near gay bars so that those numbers could be compared with those registered to students at Brigham Young University forty-five miles away.

People agreed to spy, though, because they convinced themselves they were "helping."

It was the same manipulation bishops used whenever someone came in to confess a sexual "sin." "The person you had sex with needs to repent, too. You can't be absolved if you don't help your partner in sin to repent, too. So give me the name."

Some tattling, apparently, was mandatory.

A widowed friend in my ward remarried the Relief Society president, who consistently found ways to reveal confidences that women in the ward had shared with her. Her revelations to others who had no need to know any of these secrets seemed to provide an emotional reward through shaming others.

But the passive-aggressiveness worked both ways. When the Relief Society president threw a party for select members of the congregation, one woman, who'd been close to my friend's first wife, kept "accidentally" calling the president by the wrong name.

The intentionality of the slight was clear to everyone.

Rabbi Harold Kushner wrote an insightful book called *When Bad Things Happen to Good People.* But we could just as easily write sequels: *When Good People Do Bad Things* and *When Bad People Do Good Things*.

No one's a perfect saint and no one reading this is likely 100% racist.

Still, "it's complicated" can't be an excuse for every inhumane policy or behavior, unless we want to abandon all pretense, both to ourselves and others, that we're good.

I know many kind, caring Mormons. Yet these examples aren't anomalies. Systems are in place guaranteeing such behavior in congregations across the world. We can't solve those systemic problems merely by calling out individual acts. At the same time, individuals must be accountable for their personal behavior, even if we're led to behave in certain ways by powerful, controlling systems.

Some people boldly embrace their power and corruption. That's certainly a choice we can make. But if we sincerely *want* to be good and honorable, then we must stop taking systemic reprimands personally. If we or someone on "our" side does something unacceptable, we say so, accept responsibility and, when possible, make restitution. If someone on the "other" side does something commendable, we acknowledge it. If someone on either side has a legitimate grievance, we don't suppress discussion but address the problem.

And if the offense in question is the result of a cultural norm or policy, we address the root cause.

It should not be up to others to audit our dominant culture. Because it *is* our culture, we may be blind to its faults, but once they're pointed out, it's to our own benefit to fix them. If we've moved into a majestic home in a beautiful, established neighborhood and spent several years and tens of thousands of dollars renovating the house, and then some random neighbor stops by and says, "You know, I can see from the size and position of that crack in the foundation that your front porch may fall off during a heavy thunderstorm," lashing out in anger and ordering the neighbor to leave won't alter the facts.

Blaming the subsequent collapse on the neighbor when we retell the story may help us deflect the blame, may help us feel better about our poor choice to ignore the warning, but it doesn't resolve the problem.

Some socialist organizations have homophobic policies. Some environmental groups have leaders who commit sexual improprieties. No political party, no organization, no religion can be free of members who do bad things. When we excuse bad behavior and harmful principles in the dominant culture we inhabit, when we let things slide, when we agree to be silent partners to oppression, we are not being good people.

Interesting how often "It's natural" is used to defend our inadequacies and "It's unnatural!" is used to attack our enemies.

Let's demand accountability and change within our own groups, and let's stop being accessories to the brutal crime of tribalism.

It's Their *Culture* I Don't Like

"I have nothing against Black people," I've heard white friends and relatives say. "I just don't like their culture." They might then go on to complain about teens with their pants falling down or vulgar hip hop music or women with babies fathered by different men or some other cultural "flaw."

My Mormon friends and family seem to have little difficulty with LDS leaders having children with several different women, either while married concurrently or consecutively.

But it's not only the religious who are self-righteous. When my gay friends make similar disparaging remarks about "Black culture," I point out a few issues I have with gay culture. Bitchiness might be funny in a TV series or drag show, but in real life it's just mean and petty.

Of course, there is no single "gay culture" any more than there is a monolithic Black culture. There are dozens and dozens of each. One gay friend, tired of listening to his parents moan interminably about "the gay lifestyle," responded, "You mean, going to work every day, coming home to cook dinner, watching an hour of *Law and Order*, and then going to bed to do the whole thing all over again the following day?"

"Uh…"

"Is it the *Law and Order* you find offensive? I could probably watch something different if that would help."

Some gay men demand monogamy. Others have "open" long-term relationships. Some practice polyamory. Quite a few don't want a "relationship" at all, just a strong group of friends. Some gay men have anonymous sex in bathrooms or bathhouses. Others have never set foot in a bar.

If someone hates the fact that I love other men, fine. But that alone does not describe or define my "lifestyle."

The same is true of the "African American community." There are Black people in the U.S. who don't want to be called African Americans. Others prefer the term. People may be grouped together by the larger society and end up working together in solidarity, but we can hardly forget that both Angela Davis and Herman Cain belonged to the same "community."

It's OK not to like every single thing about a group or a particular subdivision in that group. I don't even like everything about my husband. Or about myself, for that matter. How could I possibly like *everything* about *any* culture?

As Mormon missionaries in Rome, our district of six young men and four young women worked together on a "streetboard" project. Two of the missionaries were Italian, the rest Americans. As the hours passed, I realized the Americans were speaking English and completely ignoring the Italians. The Americans were also mocking aspects of the local culture quite blatantly.

I asked one of the Italian missionaries, "Le fa male sentire queste cose?"

"No, no," she said. "Sono vere."

Just trying to imagine what it must feel like to be outcasts in one's own country forced me to hear the words my friends were saying in a different context. I spent the rest of my time during that project speaking Italian with the Italians.

In Naples, one of the members who couldn't afford glasses had trouble reading the hymnbook. Already an outsider as a Mormon in Italy, she was also an outsider in her Mormon congregation because of her poor eyesight.

So I bought a notebook and wrote the words to the most popular hymns for her in large, bold markers.

It was nothing compared to the kindnesses she'd shown my companion and me. When we visited her ancient, one-room apartment with no running water, she would serve us slightly curdled milk and pieces of overripened fruit.

Some Italians were mean to me, but none ever said anything as cruel as one of my zone leaders, motioning in my direction while speaking loudly to another missionary: "Can you imagine how boring his honeymoon will be?"

Mission life isn't the joyful, spiritual experience some would lead you to believe.

I'd experienced a year-long culture shock when I arrived in Italy, adapting simultaneously to two new cultures, but when I returned to the States after my time there, I experienced culture shock all over again. Boy, Americans were weird.

I *hated* living in the suburbs, where it took forty-five minutes to walk to the nearest store. In Naples, I only had to head down to the ground floor of my building to find a paneficio. Who would ever want to live completely isolated from grocery markets and public transportation? Where was the corner bar where I could pick up some milk and cookies before bed?

Bizarre.

In English lit, when my professor asked if we understood the point of Shirley Jackson's "The Lottery," I raised my hand. "There are parts of our culture we accept without question that others would recognize instantly as horrific."

Boxing, for instance. Football with its serious brain injuries. Dog fights.

Thinking routine school massacres of children and teachers was simply the price a civilized society paid for freedom.

In grad school, we discussed adding certain previously dismissed works into "the canon." The argument was that many works by women authors over the centuries had been deemed unimportant because they dealt with "women's issues" rather than issues of literary merit, i.e., "men's issues." Black or other marginalized writers had been similarly dismissed.

One of my classmates protested any such retroactive discoveries. "I don't want to waste my time reading junk by unimportant writers."

"How do you know they're unimportant?"

"Because they're not in the canon."

As a Mormon, I'd grown up proud of our Word of Wisdom. We didn't drink or smoke. We didn't even approve of tea or coffee. We were keeping our "temples" pure.

Yet at church dances, we'd start with a prayer. "Heavenly Father, please bless these doughnuts and potato chips that they may strengthen and nourish our bodies."

Before my mission, I'd loved everything I knew about Mormon culture. Mission culture, though, was ruthlessly oppressive. Once back in America, I slowly grew to loathe the self-doubt and self-hate Mormonism taught its members, despised the judgment and condemnation it threw at both members and non-members alike, the only Christian religion that referred to Jews as gentiles.

But there are still things I find good in Mormon culture. I keep aspects of it in my life thirty-five years after leaving.

Parts of every culture are damaging while other parts are beautiful. When we focus only on the negative (or what we perceive as negative) and condemn an entire culture or an entire race or ethnicity or religion, we are, by definition, discriminating.

I used to think of Jews as a single entity. As a Christian, I had no concept of the vast differences between Orthodox, Hassidic, Conservative, or Reform Jews, no idea that even those divisions hardly began to distinguish the variety of cultures that make up Judaism.

Most Westerners don't know the difference between Shia and Sunni Muslims, much less the many other divisions among those two huge sects.

If white Americans talk about Indigenous Americans at all, they're unlikely to distinguish between Chickasaw and Lummi or even understand what the term "500 Nations" means.

Once when I was working at an adult video store, a customer came up to me, upset at a new title we'd just put out. "*Black Loads Matter*?" he protested. "White loads matter, too!" Then he stormed out of the building.

Talk about white fragility.

"I don't have anything against Black people. I just don't like their culture."

That position doesn't establish our lack of bias but instead confirms it.

I love Claudio Baglioni's music. Laura Pausini's, too. But not every single song they ever sang. We can have our likes and dislikes without being dismissive of the multitude of cultures that make up our nation and the world.

Sometimes, my friends or family will change their approach if I push back. "This isn't about race," they say. "It's their class."

Yeah, you're also not getting points for discriminating against folks with less money than you have.

"It's not about race or even class. It's just that people without an education are unpleasant to be around."

No points for that, either, I'm afraid. If educated white folks are so uncomfortable around uneducated people of any class or race, they are perfectly free to fight for tuition-free college and vocational training.

Empathy doesn't mean we like everything about a marginalized group. It doesn't mean agreement. Empathy means listening. It means not dismissing a person or entire group out of hand. It doesn't mean allowing for one or two possible exceptions to the rule. "*This* one's OK."

The astounding, normalized lack of empathy is one aspect of dominant white culture I don't like at all. But I can dislike that failing and still appreciate many other aspects of the various white cultures I know.

In fact, right now I'm off to watch another episode of *Mom*, a fun show about a group of extremely flawed white friends.

Rather than investing so much energy dismissing the cultures of others, why not improve our own, and during that never-ending process also start treating people of every other culture with a little more humanity and respect?

It's a cultural trait worth developing.

I Threw My Confederate Cap Away

I just took an internalized bias test through my workplace for the third year in a row. The results? I show a "strong preference" for white people over black, just as I have on each previous exam. I threw my Confederate cap away decades ago, but it's not as easy to get rid of the bias.

As a child, visiting my grandparents in Mississippi provided some of my best memories. Making homemade ice cream on the back steps, picking blackberries, walking the cows in for milking, swimming in the creek, shelling pecans. But life on the dairy farm wasn't all fun and games. Sometimes, the news reported sightings of bears in the area or we'd be warned to keep an eye out for black panthers. No one in the family had ever seen one, but they were the mascot for the single high school in town, so we knew they were real.

Walking with my sister through a pasture the day we heard the latest alert, I saw her stop in fear and point. "I see something black!" she said breathlessly, fixated on something moving beyond the trees along the gravel road. "It has a yellow shirt on!"

It wasn't a panther.

So we relaxed and played among the flowers, a field of Black Eyed Susans, a name I didn't learn until I was almost an adult. We'd been taught to use a racial slur to describe them. "N-word navels."

We made occasional day trips to Vicksburg, the site of some of the heaviest fighting during the Civil War. Dad bought miniature Confederate flags for my sister and me, bought us Confederate caps. Neither of my grandfathers had fought in WWII, and none of the great-grandfathers had fought in WWI, but our family had an illustrious Confederate heritage, so we ran up and down the steep hills celebrating past glory.

Back in Metairie, the middle-class suburb of New Orleans where we lived, my mother forbade me to watch the show *Julia* starring Diahann Carroll. I was also denied access later to the show *Room 222*. “It has a black person in it,” my mother explained.

At one point, my mom wanted to move back to the country and placed an ad to sell our home, describing it as “Tara-style.” It was a square brick box with brick columns, built in 1964.

One year, our family attended weekly meetings for several months to prepare for the Elks parade on Mardi Gras, the most prestigious day of the entire carnival season. We’d follow Rex down St. Charles Avenue and Canal Street. I was going to throw out beads and doubloons! The kids at school would be so jealous!

At the last minute, though, the group voted against participating. It was just too dangerous to be downtown with all those black people. They sometimes threw bottles at white people on the floats.

During my early years, Mom sometimes brought my sister and me to the French Quarter to tour the wax museum or the natural history museum. We ate beignets at the Café du Monde. We watched movies at the Robert E. Lee Theater on Robert E. Lee Boulevard, ate Italian sweets on Jefferson Davis Parkway. We passed a statue of General Beauregard on our visits to Storyland in City Park. Sometimes, we shopped along Canal Street. Those adventures all ended once there were "too many black people." My parents did permit me to go down to Lee Circle on Mardi Gras with my best friend and his mom, as long as I promised to be careful. Black people sometimes put razor blades on the tips of their shoes and kicked white people. Best if I wore boots for extra protection.

My suburban public school wasn't integrated until I reached fifth grade. By the time I reached ninth grade, my parents put my sister and me in a private Baptist school that banned blacks. "We're not prejudiced," the headmistress explained. "We just don't approve of interracial dating."

One of my classmates was a David Duke fan. The head of the KKK lived only a mile from the school. Several of my other classmates encouraged the rest of us not to elect the lone Hispanic girl in our class as one of the cheerleaders.

But at home I defiantly watched shows like *Good Times* and *The Jeffersons*. I wasn't prejudiced. Racism was stupid.

Though my parents had both grown up Baptist, we'd all converted to Mormonism in 1971, and in June of 1978, the Prophet announced a new revelation. Black men were now “allowed” to hold the priesthood. The only local news affiliate to cover the story was WDSU. “They’re owned by blacks,” my mom explained in a what-can-you-expect tone.

My mom sounds like a horrible person, and her racism was clearly destructive. But growing up with her was a mostly wonderful experience. That’s a large part of why “good” people harboring terrible prejudices don’t see themselves as “bad.” It’s almost as if racists like my mother have Multiple Personality Disorder. 97 of their personalities are good, upstanding people. It’s the remaining 3 who are criminally insane. But it’s too uncomfortable to rehabilitate those three, so the other 97 simply go into denial.

It’s not unlike what a friend of mine coping with schizophrenia has had to endure throughout her life, mean voices in her head telling her things that aren’t true, making her and everyone around her miserable until she was finally able to start treating her disease.

When I turned nineteen, it was time for me to “serve” as a volunteer missionary for two years. Mormons have no say over where they’re sent, so waiting for “the call” to arrive in the mail was excruciating. What if I were sent someplace boring? Or scary? One of my aunt’s boyfriends had gone to Japan. The man she eventually married had served in Finland. When my letter arrived from Salt Lake, I ran upstairs and opened it.

When I came back down, my mother's brows furrowed. "Where are you going?" She pressed her lips together to prepare herself for the bad news.

"It's someplace that has food you really like."

My mother's shoulders slumped. "Mexico," she said, shaking her head slowly. "You're going to Mexico."

"It's someplace *else* that has food you like."

My mother's eyes lit up. Then she started jumping up and down, clapping. "You're going to Italy! You're going to Italy!"

Everyone at church was excited, too. "Oh, you'll get to learn Spanish," they said.

"Uh, no, I think they speak Italian in Italy."

"Be careful with the water. You don't want to get sick."

Italy was wonderful and miserable and incredible and depressing, the negatives largely a result of the oppressive missionary lifestyle. Every moment of our lives was regimented, our actions constantly monitored.

In my first area, a young local member, a carabiniere, was so excited to learn I was from New Orleans that he struggled valiantly to blurt out, "South rise again!" in English far better than my Italian. Perhaps I should have found it strange, but one of the songs we had learned in Culture Capsule back in the Missionary Training Center was "Zip-a-Dee-Doo-Dah" in Italian, so perhaps not. My first four assignments were as companion to various district leaders, the position jokingly referred to as "District N-word."

Told every day our lack of faith and success was a disappointment to God, I became suicidal for the first time in my life and wanted desperately to go home. Of course, doing so would have labeled me a failure among other Mormons for the remainder of my life. My mother, eager to help, wrote back after my latest unhappy letter. "If you want to come home," she said, "I'll hide you in the attic."

I plodded on, and my time in Italy became a transformative experience. I saw abject poverty for the first time. I witnessed a kidnapping near the train station in Rome. I was caught in a Camorra gang war in Naples. Teens threw heavy rocks at us because they hated Americans. I was spit on and kicked, chased with garden shears, had guns pulled on me. I was approached by dozens and dozens of "gypsies." A woman asked me to marry her daughter and bring her to the U.S.

I met folks from Ghana and Nigeria and Somalia. An African woman the sister missionaries were teaching was abducted. We never saw her again.

And then I returned to Metairie, struggling with culture shock in my conservative, white neighborhood as I began my sophomore year at the University of New Orleans.

When I saw a young man on campus I'd known growing up, I was surprised to realize for the first time that he was black. I'd always been confused at how different he looked from everyone else in the family, but it had never occurred to me he wasn't white until I saw him in a different setting.

I returned to Italy a year later, becoming engaged to a former Italian sister missionary I'd worked with who was a Communist. We agreed I should complete my degree in America before we married, and then I'd move back to Italy and teach English.

I absolutely loved literature. Jane Austen, Charles Dickens, Thomas Hardy, Edgar Allan Poe, Nathaniel Hawthorne, and more. I even liked Shakespearean sonnets and Middle English lit.

My Chaucer professor chastised the class one day for laughing at a story from the Canterbury Tales in which townspeople blamed the bubonic plague on Jews. "Medieval people were so stupid," a student said.

"You don't think people today bear illogical prejudices against certain groups?" the professor asked pointedly.

Years later, I wasn't surprised to run into my professor in a gay bookstore with his black partner.

At church, the first black man in our congregation was ordained a high priest, the most prestigious position at the local level. My father still used the N-word every time he spoke of the man, and he laughed every time I corrected him. I asked another high priest if he felt any of the others in the group were prejudiced. "No," he said. "We believe in equality."

"So you wouldn't mind if your son married Brother Alfonse's daughter?"

"Well, we don't approve of interracial marriage, of course, but that doesn't mean we're bigoted."

How blind, I wondered, could these people be? Thank God *I* wasn't biased.

As I approached graduation, I realized I still hadn't managed to change my sexual orientation, despite my continued virginal status. The first mission clearly hadn't been enough of a sacrifice for Heavenly Father to heal me. So I talked to my bishop and stake president about serving a second two-year mission. I talked to my fiancée about it.

She wasn't happy. But if I needed to marry a woman, I had to become straight first, not "hope" it would happen miraculously sometime after.

And if worse came to worst, at least missionary life was the closest I could get to marriage with another man.

I finally broke up with my fiancée after I realized I was always going to be gay. I came out while in grad school, was called to a Court of Love, and was excommunicated, my stake president and other members of the High Council telling me I'd denied the Holy Ghost and betrayed God.

It wasn't until that evening, when I heard one of the high councilmen refer to me as "articulate" that I understood my own problematic use of the word when talking about "educated" blacks. The slur in my case meant, "when they are learned they think they are wise."

It meant something different for black people but was equally insulting, perhaps more infuriating because the white people like me using it thought we were saying something "nice."

My excommunication was announced during church services. Friends I'd known for years refused to talk to me.

But I felt genuinely free and soon met my first lover. We lived in a mobile home in St. Rose on the edge of the swamp past the airport. Everyone in the neighborhood lived in trailers and mobile homes.

Everyone was white.

Well, almost everyone. One day, two white neighbors stopped by our place. "We just told that guy down the street he'd better have that black guy staying with him move out or we'd burn them out." The men laughed. "What do you think about *that*?"

I could hardly say what I was really thinking: "Sure, the two faggots out here in the boondocks are thrilled to hear your violent, bigoted threats."

We decided to move to the Marigny, just outside the French Quarter. There I noticed the neighborhood public schools always kept their classroom windows open in the sweltering heat and humidity. My elementary school in Jefferson Parish had air conditioning twenty-five years earlier, but schools in Orleans Parish still didn't. And I'd never known that until I was almost thirty.

Nearly every public school in New Orleans had a mostly black student body, almost half the schools named after a "generous" slave owner. Virtually every white public school student attended a magnet school for the "gifted." Nearly all the remaining white kids attended a variety of private Catholic schools or a single private school serving mostly Jewish students.

My first teaching job was at SUNO—Southern University at New Orleans. It was a public university, historically black like its sister campus in Baton Rouge. This was the 1990s, and the mostly black SUNO and mostly white UNO sat hardly a mile apart, two public universities still quite separate and not equal.

For the next ten years, I taught evening classes at SUNO, all the while thinking I wasn't prejudiced, every semester learning I still was. Some of that realization, unfortunately, didn't take place until years after I left campus. Looking back, I squirm at some of the things I did and said. I made a particularly awkward comment once in response to a general rebellion over the amount of homework I assigned. "We work during the day, Mr. Townsend. We don't have time to read all this stuff."

"You people," I said. I'd meant it as "you students," but boy, I sure learned something that evening.

Almost every semester, an angry student would meet with me after class. "You can't give me a D on this paper! I'm a high school English teacher!"

I was told by the assistant dean, "You're penalizing the students for being black. You need to understand the background of your students and take that into account when you grade." While three major grammar errors would fail a paper at the University of New Orleans, where I also taught, students could have fifteen at SUNO, and I was still expected to award a passing grade. But after I complied, the assistant dean called me back to her office. "You're trying to keep the students ignorant and keep them in their place!"

In class, we sometimes discussed current topics related to race, and when the Rodney King riots erupted in Los Angeles, one student defended an attack on a white woman, married to a black man, dragged out of her car. My student felt that every white person got what they deserved. When a young white woman, an American college student, was killed by a mob in a South African township where she'd been registering people to vote, one of my students said, "White people always think we need their help. They were right to kill her."

On my way to work one evening, I heard about the Oklahoma City bombing on the radio and upon arrival asked the assistant dean if she'd heard the news. She ignored me, so I thought I hadn't spoken loudly enough and repeated the question.

"Maybe the FBI did it!" she finally spat at me. I walked to my class stunned. I hadn't yet heard of the MOVE firebombing several years earlier.

I received perhaps a dozen pieces of hate mail in my office mailbox one semester. One note simply declared, "The White Man is the Devil," but most of the letters were long rants. I tried comparing the handwriting on the notes with that of the essays by my students, but I could never find a match. I even compared the handwriting with that of the assistant dean, who'd told me flat out, "I think you're a racist, and I'm going to do everything I can to get rid of you." It wasn't her handwriting, either.

The moment the dean retired, the assistant dean got her wish, and I was no longer an instructor in the Evening and Weekend College. The truth is… the assistant dean was right about me. I have no doubt I said and did racist things I don't even remember now because I was unaware of their significance and impact. It never occurred to me to study racism because I was convinced I wasn't racist and therefore had no personal behavior or mindset to change. Even in an atmosphere that offered ample evidence to the contrary, I'd chosen to remain ignorant that such a thing as structural racism even existed, much less that I had an obligation to help dismantle it. At the time, I was relieved not to be rehired after the new dean took over. I'd no longer have to face feeling so uncomfortable every day.

Only I did.

The staff in a store on the "black" side of St. Claude refused to wait on me. Once, when I honked impatiently at a car taking too long to turn on Elysian Fields, the black driver made a U-turn and chased me for blocks. I gave up driving, recognizing my growing irritation with traffic wasn't going to improve. I soon found myself almost always the lone white passenger on public transportation. My family was aghast that I'd deliberately *chosen* to do something so reckless and dangerous. I only saw a single white driver in all the years I rode the bus around New Orleans.

A priest walking his dog one night two blocks from my Marigny apartment was shot and killed by a black man during a mugging. A woman jogging a block past that was shot by a black man during her morning jog. A tourist at a bed and breakfast two blocks in another direction was shot and killed by a black man. A friend of mine was murdered in his Marigny apartment by a black man. Another man was found tied to a chair in his apartment after a black man broke in. A man was seriously injured and his wife killed by a black man during a home invasion six doors down from me. Two of my friends were beaten in the French Quarter by black men. Another had his ribs fractured in a mugging Uptown. A white woman I knew was attacked stepping out of her car.

I understood by this point that white people had ensured a black underclass trapped in poverty with limited access to good education and decent jobs. But that didn't keep me from crossing the street when I saw a black man walking down the sidewalk.

Another friend was murdered by a white man during a gay bashing. But in my mind, the killer wasn't "white." He was a "religious homophobe."

One of my white coworkers looked hauntingly like Jeffrey Dahmer. I gasped when I saw him out on Mardi Gras day, leading his black lover around on a chain through the French Quarter.

Another coworker told me he was hoping to get into med school based on his minority status. "What minority are you?" I asked.

"I'm black."

One of my fuck buddies complained once about the extra layer of discrimination he faced as part of two oppressed groups. "What's the other group?" I asked.

"I'm black."

I'm not colorblind. I'm simply inattentive. I didn't even notice my husband had blue eyes until we'd been together two years. And in New Orleans, "black" covered a wide variety of skin tones.

Do I have any bias, any internalized white superiority?

Of course I do! How could I not? I recognize I must constantly and actively combat it every single day.

I learned in a History of the English Language course that the names of some towns in England are of Celtic origin, going back as far as 800 BCE. Some names still exist from inhabitants living on the British Isles even before the Celts. The residents since then have resisted any alteration in the names despite influxes of Angles, Saxons, Jutes, and Normans. "Place names are very resistant to change," my professor explained.

But a simple stroll through the French Quarter of New Orleans showed me that change was possible. Ursulines Avenue used to be named Calle del Arsenal. Governor Nicholls bore the prior name of Calle del Hospital. Decatur Street had previously been named Camino Real y Muelle at one point and Rue de la Levee at another. And Jackson Square had first been Plaza d'Armas.

Working on my genealogy as a teen, I learned the 1850 census was the gold standard for information. I was confused at first to discover that the area my ancestors had lived in almost since their arrival in Mississippi had originally been named Lawrence County. I'd only known it as Lincoln County. Obviously, though, it would not have been named that before the Civil War. Yet despite my family's continued racism, no one seemed to suffer unduly because of the renaming.

Mormons do genealogy so we can perform "proxy work" in temples and baptize our ancestors posthumously. In a university library, I discovered a letter from one of my great-great-grandfathers who fought at the battle of Vicksburg, in which he petitioned his commanding officer to transfer him away from the fighting because he had hemorrhoids. We were all so happy to know he was now Mormon in heaven.

Andrew Jackson was the president who'd signed the Indian Removal Act of 1830, opening the land now known as Mississippi to my ancestors, who all arrived within the following decade. The capital of Mississippi is, unsurprisingly, named after him.

Many among my family and friends talked of Confederate symbols as part of their "heritage." But since the Confederacy only existed for five years, what they're really celebrating is the white supremacy that both pre- and post-dated the Civil War.

Almost all of my white friends and family, like me, never felt they were prejudiced. Some still adamantly deny it. But if we can't make the most minor effort to change the names of a few streets and university buildings, relocate a few statues to museums, and agree that naming military bases after traitors was a mistake that must be both repudiated and rectified, then our "lack" of prejudice doesn't mean very much.

The problem, of course, is that most white conservatives *don't* think the Confederates were traitors. I'm well aware of how these folks *do* treat traitors.

And I can guarantee they're not waxing nostalgic over me.

After Hurricane Katrina, I relocated to the Pacific Northwest, but on a return visit to New Orleans, I heard the daughter of one of my friends talk about her work with the National Guard immediately after the storm. She was assigned to make sure everyone evacuated. "This one old black man wouldn't leave," she said. "He wanted to stay in his house." She shook her head. "He told me, 'You can't make me leave,' so I told him, 'I can shoot you if you don't.'"

She thought this was a funny anecdote.

After several weeks of Black Lives Matter protests, after taking several more online courses on bias and diversity through my employer in addition to the in-person workshops I participated in over the two preceding years, I was unhappy to discover that my latest internalized bias test still shows I have a "strong preference" for white people over black. If I keep taking this test every year for the rest of my life, I'm not sure the results will ever change much. Maybe, if I continue to work at it, my score may eventually evolve to, "slight preference."

The least we can do as "good" white people, and I mean absolutely the very least, is remove monuments to racism from public spaces and rename the streets, university buildings, and military bases honoring those who caused so much suffering and death to our fellow citizens.

If farmers in Mississippi, middle-class churchgoers in Metairie, and so many other white people can still feel the sting of losses incurred over a five-year period more than 150 years ago, can we not manage to feel the slightest empathy for folks who have suffered continually for more than 400 years?

We must make this small token of repentance immediately so we can move on to dismantling more serious aspects of structural and institutional racism.

But that's the reason for so much resistance to taking *any* step, isn't it? We want to think we've already arrived at our destination, and we dread acknowledging we haven't, because the rest of that road looks steeper than a hill in Vicksburg, and we know there is no place to rest along the way.

Our journey doesn't have to be a Trail of Tears, though, or a Middle Passage. It can be a Path to Reconciliation, a double-laned highway to both secular and religious morality.

Because while the road to Hell may be paved with good intentions, the signs pointing the way are posted by resentment and a refusal to accept the truth.

So let's choose to march—humbly, haltingly, boldly, however we can—toward equity.

Throwing away our bias may be harder even than losing the weight we gained eating Grandma's homemade pecan pie.

But justice is a choice. And we can make it.

Facing Our Biases without Self-Loathing

Remember in high school when our English teacher wanted us to read Shakespeare? Perhaps she had us read *Romeo and Juliet*, hoping it would be less painful. But nope, it was excruciating. Or how about when our history teacher had us do a report on the Great Depression? Boring.

For many people, learning about our country's tradition of inequality isn't only emotionally threatening but also promises to be dreadfully tedious, just like almost every other assignment to "learn something important." But there are ways to make the venture less intimidating, so we don't have to fear being tested on our new knowledge or expected to act on it immediately.

"White fragility" may feel like an offensive term, but it's not inaccurate. Still, if we are sincere about addressing injustice, we need to find ways to progress without shattering our sense of self-worth. Perhaps folks facing daily oppression won't approve of this slower approach, and certainly, if we *can* learn faster, we should, but slow is better than total avoidance.

A tortoise *can* make it to the finish line.

As we learn more, hopefully we'll want to speed up our learning. And I expect most of us have already done some work. We'd simply benefit from confronting our biases more systematically.

In our current fast-paced world, the easiest and least threatening way to learn about bias is through film. And a good way to use film is to watch something with an indirect approach to bias. We don't watch *To Sir, with Love* to understand racism better. We watch because it's a moving account of teaching working class students in London. We don't watch *The Crying Game* to understand trans women better. We watch because it's a captivating story about an IRA terrorist trying to atone for killing a British soldier. We don't watch *Professor Marston and the Wonder Women* to learn about polyamory. We watch because it's a fascinating biopic about the creators of the superhero Wonder Woman.

Those who can't yet bring themselves to devote two hours to the subject of bias should probably start out on YouTube. Hundreds of TED talks and other short videos lasting no more than ten minutes can offer us small doses of understanding and can be fit into almost anyone's schedule. Our first venture into context doesn't have to be watching the entire mini-series of Alex Hailey's *Roots.* We can watch a ten-minute video today, another video two days from now, and the next one three days after that. Since it's easy to forget the importance of continued learning, however, we need to put learning on our schedules, sending ourselves reminders from our phone or email.

Date Night can be sitting back with a bowl of popcorn to watch *Black Panther*. It can be Family Night sitting down with the kids to watch Disney's *The Princess and the Frog.* Let's throw out the idea we must be masochists to learn. And if we want to study without letting our friends and family know, that's OK, too.

We can focus on just one historically oppressed group at a time or mix and match. There's no need to compare whose suffering was worst. There may well be a "winner" in such a contest, but all forms of oppression need to be addressed. Let's start where we are and move forward.

When we transition from short YouTube videos or short articles to feature-length films, we sometimes face the same challenge we did in high school—many "important" films are boring, or at least, the subject matter alone threatens us with tedium, making us less likely to turn on a movie we might actually enjoy. Fortunately, the material to access is so abundant we can surely find some movies or books that suit our individual tastes. "Best of" lists are everywhere.

When we're ready to get serious about confronting our biases, though, we may as well start with *Older than America*. If we can't get past the misinformation we've been taught about the earliest colonizers and subsequent encounters between Europeans and Native Americans, we'll never be able to see beyond our front door. Many of these films still have a white POV, but some to consider are *Reel Injun*, *The Mission*, *Smoke Signals*, *Trail of Tears*, and *Bury My Heart at Wounded Knee.* Typing "Native American history" in the Search bar on YouTube will offer us dozens of short mini-lessons.

We can set aside one evening a week for School Night, a dedicated time for learning. It needn't always be about bias. Perhaps just one School Night a month will touch on that. If other nights focus on astronomy or art or another subject, we can still sneak in something like *Hidden Figures* or *Floyd Norman: An Animated Life* once in a while.

Tootsie and *Bend it Like Beckham* are comedies but still convey important information about sexism. We can start with lighter films like these, but we should schedule weightier material down the line, not leaving it up to chance. We could put *Made in Dagenham* on our schedule for next month. Then *Suffragette* and *Half the Picture* and *Bombshell*. Jodie Foster in *The Accused* is a complicated character who shows us that even if a woman is dressed provocatively, flirtatious, drunk or high, it's still rape if the guy forces himself on her. The series based on Margaret Atwood's work, *The Handmaid's Tale*, may be fictional, but we'll understand oppression better if we realize every atrocity in the show has already been perpetrated in real life on an oppressed group somewhere. Any time we're feeling overwhelmed, we can go back to mixing in some comedies. If we reach a place where our only new study is always something heavy, we'll just stop doing it altogether. Let's try to throw in some foreign films, too, like *Volver* or *Palabi Kothae*, kind of a Bangladeshi version of the comedy *9 to 5*. My best teachers always made learning fun, even if the subject was difficult.

We must accept our emotional limitations if we're going to deal realistically with the problem of our own ignorance, taking our own storytelling preferences into consideration. But it might be useful to develop a written plan or schedule. If we wait until we're "in the mood" before looking for titles, it'll be a struggle every single time, and the opportunity will slip away more often than not. We owe it to ourselves to make learning this essential information something we're willing to do despite our weaknesses. No one stays on a healthy diet if they're miserable at every meal. If they don't plan ahead, they'll end up eating whatever's left in the fridge.

In and Out stars Kevin Kline and Joan Cusack in delightful performances. *Pride* has lots of gay characters, but it's "about" raising money to support striking coal miners. *I Love You Phillip Morris* is a dark comedy starring Jim Carrey as a gay convict. The mini-series *A Very English Scandal*, starring Hugh Grant as a real-life British politician, is morbidly funny, outrageous, filled with extremely flawed characters, yet we still leave feeling a bit more compassion for the oppressed, more understanding about how that oppression often leads us to make terrible choices. *Beautiful Thing* is a simple, sweet movie about working class teens in the UK. So what if we have to struggle a little with the regional accent?

We don't have to go into this self-education feeling an obligation to accept the morality of any sexual behavior or political position that our religion or culture has condemned. We don't have to *like* LGBTQ folks to know that understanding more about them is essential in today's society. We can read and watch and listen just for the purpose of understanding. I can watch a show about the Vatican without feeling obligated to convert. *The Celluloid Closet* is fascinating simply as film history. The Oscar-winning documentary *The Times of Harvey Milk* is both educational and entertaining. And the part of the film where we see a candlelight march with 50,000 people stretching block after block the evening of the assassination, followed by riots the evening the murderer is given a light sentence, can perhaps help us understand some of the motivation for riots that take place in the Black Lives Matter movement.

Selma doesn't need to feel like a school assignment. It's a genuinely good film about a pivotal moment in U.S. history. *The Hate U Give* may not be everybody's first choice for films on police killings, but it's well-made, and it's not boring. *The Color Purple* starring Whoopi Goldberg was nominated for 11 Academy Awards. We're not going to suffer sitting through it. Some lighter African American movies include *Barbershop*, *Akeelah and the Bee*, and *Sorry to Bother You.* But let's face it. To understand even a fraction of the devastating racist legacy of our nation, we'll need to watch a few "difficult" films, too. So let's schedule *Detroit* and *13th* and *The Last Black Man in San Francisco* and, yes, even *12 Years a Slave* and *Amistad.* Henry Louis Gates, Jr., has made some fascinating documentaries, too.

Four hours of *Schindler's List* sounds more tedious than Tolstoy's *War and Peace*. But it's a compelling film directed by Steven Spielberg. It's important to see if we're to be culturally literate, and if we thought the shower scene in Hitchcock's *Psycho* was unforgettable, we'll be shaken to our core to watch characters we've spent three hours getting to know being herded into the showers at

Auschwitz. Yes, we'll be uncomfortable watching, but it's just a few hours out of our lives, not the centuries of pogroms and mass murder these families have faced.

It's OK to be uncomfortable for a brief period to understand the misery others have endured far longer. *Hotel Rwanda* and other movies or mini-series made and set outside the U.S. help us to develop a more global view of bias and discrimination in a variety of forms. They'll help us put our own in perspective. Sweden's *Miss Friman's War*, Italy's *Luisa Spagnoli*, and Denmark's *The New Nurses* are popular shows in Europe. Watching them isn't a chore. Neither is learning from them.

What's important about this self-education is acknowledging upfront we won't be able to unsee what we've seen. We cannot see *Triangle Fire* without forever viewing workers' rights in a different light.

And deep down, we all understand this is the very reason we keep putting off addressing the various biases we harbor. We're afraid we'll be expected to change, not just by others but by *ourselves*. And change is scary, especially if what needs changing is part of our worldview.

But unless we sincerely believe we are already 100% perfect in every way, let's at least commit to watching a handful of short videos in the privacy of our own home when no one else is around. Once we realize we won't crumble into heaps of self-loathing, we can watch a few more, read a short article or two. Whether we like or fully understand the differences between people living in our country, even in our own families, we must find a way to work together. Or face another 400 years of conflict.

Surely, indefinite division and hatred and hurt isn't *really* what we want for ourselves and our families.

Maya Angelou said that when we know better, we do better.

Let's accept that we've all made mistakes out of ignorance. It's impossible not to. No one is born knowing everything. But we have a chance now to address some of that ignorance safely, quietly, in a way that doesn't threaten our self-respect.

But, for God's sake, let's not invalidate the work we're doing by telling those in oppressed groups all about our "growth." If a coworker confides she has breast cancer, we don't tell her about our grandmother or cousin or next-door neighbor who had cancer, how they dealt with it, and the outcome. It's an almost instinctive way to react, but the conversation should be focused on our coworker. Watching a video or two on what *not* to say to folks who are suffering would help people in almost *every* relationship.

We owe a committed approach to facing our biases to African Americans, to Native Americans, Asian Americans, Persian Americans, Arab Americans, LGBTQ folks, Dravidians, and everyone else. We won't stop being ourselves just because we know more about others.

But we don't owe this work only to our fellow citizens. We owe it to ourselves as well.

Learn the Truth: Facing Revisionist History

Many years ago when I told some Mormon friends I'd met D. Michael Quinn, one of them said, with a mixture of condescension and disgust, "He writes revisionist history, right?" My friend used the term to mean "rewriting history to fit his agenda." The truth was that Quinn revealed facts that had been deliberately hidden by LDS Church leaders. One of those leaders, Apostle Boyd K. Packer, had told him to his face, "I have a hard time with historians because they idolize the truth. The truth is not uplifting," and said publicly not long afterward, "Some things that are true are not very useful."

Many Mormons, other Christian evangelicals, and political conservatives in general fear revisionist history not because it isn't "uplifting," and not because it isn't "very useful" to their conservative agenda, but largely because it reveals they've spent a lifetime believing lies. No one wants to face that.

Go to any ex-Mormon or ex-Jehovah's Witnesses online discussion and the first thing you'll notice is how *angry* folks are when they discover they've dedicated the past twenty or thirty years to organizations they now feel have lied to them. Some of these former believers move on to other faiths, some work through their anger in a few years, and some remain angry for decades.

One woman in her sixties, dismayed to discover her entire life had been devoted to sustaining a lie, wasn't angry. She instead felt deeply saddened, mourning both the loss of her faith and the sixty years she could never get back.

I believed in Santa Claus until I was thirteen. Two or three years earlier, when I'd begun doubting and asked my mother to be honest with me, she'd assured me Santa was real, and I continued believing for a while longer. I felt she wouldn't lie to me if I was direct. She felt that if I was asking, then I still wanted to believe.

What I felt was betrayed when I finally realized the truth.

And this was just over a silly children's story I should have been able to figure out much sooner on my own.

As Americans, we've been taught our entire lives that Columbus was a great man. As Mormons, we were even taught that he was divinely inspired, the fulfilment of Book of Mormon prophecy, and a blessing to the native inhabitants of the Americas. So when we read that he was a brutal monster who enslaved and tortured and killed thousands of indigenous people, we don't want to hear it. It must be a lie. It's "revisionist" history.

The facts are well-documented. Just because we were denied those facts doesn't stop them from being true. And it certainly doesn't prevent other people from knowing they're real.

My first few years after returning to New Orleans from my mission, I listened to tapes of the San Remo music festival and other Italian pop. Fiordaliso would sing "Una sporca poesia" and I'd marvel at her use of metaphors. "Il capolinea del cuore" and "trucco la faccia dell'anima mia" were beautiful phrases.

Zucchero sang about "Una notte che vola via."

And some incredible singer with the clearest voice imaginable asked me, night after night, "Tu cosa fai stasera?"

I fantasized for months, for years, about returning to Italy, hiding from the people who knew me as an upstanding young Mormon, and sharing my life with an Italian man who spoke no English.

I wanted to rewrite my personal history. Revise the future prescribed for me.

As a gay man, I've heard many stories of parents who saw their children as strangers when they learned the truth. "I don't know who you are anymore!"

To be honest, we often struggle to discover who we really are, too. Some folks who come out late mourn the loss of decades of authentic life, just as the woman who left Mormonism in her sixties.

It's a similar feeling when parents learn their infants were switched at birth or when adult children discover they were adopted. One Jewish woman whose friends joked that she "looked" black was dismayed to learn she truly was of African descent.

Husbands or wives in monogamous relationships are heartbroken when they discover their spouse has been cheating on them, not just once but for the past ten or fifteen years.

It's devastating to discover you've been duped, especially by someone you love.

I spent decades enjoying the 1939 classic *The Wizard of Oz.* I hated learning that Judy Garland was given drugs during the filming so she could keep up with the long hours. I hated discovering that the producer bullied and threatened her. I hated learning that Margaret Hamilton's third-degree burns were ignored while Billie Burke's cold was attended to.

Reality was ruining the many years of wonderful memories and feelings I associated with this film.

"The truth is not uplifting."

Then I learned that some of the actors portraying the Munchkins were Jews who escaped Nazi Germany by going to America to appear in the film.

Lesbian comedian Wanda Sykes was not happy to learn some of her Black ancestors were slaveowners.

Kevin Bacon wasn't happy to learn he was a victim of Bernie Madoff's Ponzi scheme. It would have been far better if the theft had never occurred. But since it *did* happen, wasn't it better to know?

I talked to Duane Mitchell not long after he read my book about the Upstairs Lounge. He'd asked his mother repeatedly over the years to tell him more about his father, but all she would ever say was, "Your father was a drunk and he died in a bar!"

Duane was in his fifties before he learned more of the story. His father, "Mitch," had been socializing at the Upstairs with his lover, Horace, and several friends from church when an arsonist set the place on fire.

Mitch was one of several who escaped out a back exit but then realized Horace was still inside. He ran back into the flames to find him.

Both Mitch and Horace died that evening.

Duane and his brother, ten and eleven at the time, were visiting from another state and had been dropped off at a movie theater while Mitch and Horace went to the French Quarter. The boys waited throughout the night for their father and his "roommate" to come pick them up, watching Disney's *The World's Greatest Athlete* seven times, until their father's landlady and the police came to pick them up in the morning.

Perhaps Mitch wasn't perfect. Who is? And the truth was certainly not fun for Duane to hear.

But it mattered.

The truth hurts. It also heals. It can kill. And it can save.

The truth itself is neutral. And when it does hurt, it's almost always the preceding lies that are actually causing the pain.

We don't need our heroes to be perfect, but if they're downright horrible, perhaps we shouldn't insist they remain our heroes.

We can cry over our lost hero Columbus. Or we can use the information to lift still-oppressed indigenous peoples.

We can cry over our lost faith. Or we can decide to show compassion for others because loving our neighbors as ourselves is a good principle no matter where it comes from.

We can cry over our lost Tooth Fairy. Or we can work to include dental care in a universal healthcare program.

But let's be honest, just because we can turn our pain into progress doesn't mean that learning the truth isn't sometimes still legitimately painful.

It might help, though, to decide what we want to be true about ourselves—are we the type of person who would continue telling lies just to protect ourselves, even knowing those lies hurt others?

Or are we the kind of person who believes "the truth shall set you free"?

Is Critical Race Theory 'True'?

Growing up Mormon, every time I encountered "anti-Mormon" information, I was told, "It's from a non-member" or "It's from an ex-Mormon." This was always followed with, "Who are you going to believe? If you want to know about chemistry, you ask a chemist. If you want to know about running, you ask a runner. If you want to know about Mormons, you ask a Mormon."

This made perfect sense. Anyone who wasn't Mormon could easily have an agenda. It could be sour grapes if they'd been excommunicated. They could be trying to make the LDS Church look bad for other reasons. They could simply be mistaken. After all, if they had never even been Mormon, could they really know what they were talking about?

But too many of my Mormon friends and family don't grant the same degree of authority to others. Who better to inform us about racism, for instance, than those who have been oppressed by it? Instead, we rail against the "dangers" of Critical Race Theory. We flatly refuse to examine the facts.

Of course, not every purported "fact" these days is true. As Mark Hofmann showed members of the LDS Church, not even every historical document is real. We should question and verify any new information that feels threatening.

But questioning isn't the same as blatantly denying reality. The evidence detailing systemic racism is overwhelming.

Often, when we as white folks finally do try to address it, we're warned, "Be prepared to feel uncomfortable." That does little other than make us want to retreat immediately.

I know people who walk out of a room any time an awkward scene comes up on TV, even in a comedy. No one likes feeling uncomfortable.

And, perhaps worse, addressing racism is also *inconvenient*.

Recently, some coworkers asked me to join an Anti-Racist Book Club that would meet twice a month. Unfortunately, the meetings would be held Friday afternoons, on my day off. I didn't want to be tied down during my few hours of freedom.

Yet what was the alternative? I couldn't attend meetings during a work shift.

We can't solve a centuries-old problem with thoughts and prayers alone. So I made a modest effort and joined the book club. Many others are taking similar tentative steps.

So now we've buckled down and are finally engaged. And *then* we hear some Black activists claim that everything a white person does, even efforts at anti-racism, is self-serving. We're just trying to feel good about ourselves.

Well, of *course* we are. *Everyone* wants to feel good about themselves. We do it by telling people our religion is best. Or our race. Or our country.

Or our political party.

Whatever it takes, right?

I accept accusations of selfishness and ignorance and imperfections of all kinds because those accusations are true.

But doing anti-racist work is still important for me as a white man because *I* benefit from living in a society that is increasingly just and equitable.

Some of my Black coworkers say, "We didn't create structural racism. It's not *our* job to dismantle it."

And white coworkers say the same thing. "*I* didn't create this. Why is it *my* job to fix it?"

The truth is it is your responsibility. And it's mine. It's the responsibility of everyone who wants to be a decent human being.

Because decent human beings fight injustice. They're at least willing to examine the evidence.

A friend once told me about the breakup of her marriage. "I complained that he wasn't willing to make a single change I'd asked for. And do you know what he said? 'Why should I make any changes? *I'm* getting what I want.'"

It's clear that many white folks don't want to make changes because "the system" benefits us, even imperfectly, as is.

We regularly hear that "most people are just doing the best they can." But it isn't true. I'm not doing the best I can. I'm doing as much as I'm willing. I hope to increase what I'm willing to do but I'm definitely not doing my best yet. That's the privilege of having privilege.

So, should white people open ourselves to the examination of structural and systemic racism? Should Mormons?

If we think we're already living in the promised peace of the Millennium, perhaps we don't need to.

But if we want to experience any peace in the meantime, we'd better start doing the work necessary to achieve it.

Racist Gods

Ever seen one of those signs at work, "X days since last accident"?

How about the signs at church "X days since last sin"?

What was the longest stretch of days you were perfect, without a single sin during an entire 24-hour span?

63?

47?

2?

None?

No one likes facing their faults. I'm irritated when someone points out I've interrupted them while they were speaking. In response, I want to tell them they were taking too long to make their point, or that they'd already made it, or that they'd interrupted me just two minutes earlier.

The truth is I'm mad because they're right. After years of being a mousy wallflower, I finally learned to be more assertive and participate in discussions. This was supposed to be a good thing. But now I go too far and have to consciously hold back. I've done something rude by interrupting, even if unintentionally, and I hate realizing I still make these mistakes, despite years of concerted effort.

Likewise, most white religious conservatives are not open to considering we might possess a serious moral failing we've been unaware of our whole lives. We spend years putting our plastic into recycling bins and then learn that almost no plastic is ever recycled. We thought we were *good*, and now we discover we've been contributing to a terrible problem all along without meaning to.

Having good intentions doesn't change the negative impact we make.

Most white people know we don't "get it" when it comes to racism. And it's human nature to dismiss what we don't understand. "I'll never need this stupid algebra just to work as a cook." "If I'm studying to be a nurse, why do I have to read Shakespeare?" "I'm Jewish. Why should I care what Baptists believe?"

My Mormon friends and family have an added challenge in addressing what we see as a "new" problem with our character. We base our lives on the doctrine that the ultimate commandment is to "Be ye therefore perfect." We're here to be tested, be purified, and become gods ourselves after Judgment Day.

Yet, even with this powerful self-concept, even as we plan to rule over our own worlds, we're so fragile we can't accept we might actually need to make a few additional changes to our behavior, ask a few questions, do a little research.

As a Mormon missionary in Italy, I was told, "You're here to teach, not to learn." We were special, the Marines of the missionary force, because we'd been sent right to Satan's doorstep to do spiritual battle with the Whore of Babylon. I knew nothing of Roman emperors, nothing of

Mussolini, fascism, and the battles of WWII. I was taught nothing about Catholicism in preparation for my assignment.

I was expected to reach the hearts and souls of the Italian people without knowing the most basic information about them.

We had the truth, after all, and it wasn't audacious to say so. It wasn't our fault we were right and they were wrong. Those were the "facts." We'd have told the Pope to his face if we could have gotten an audience with him. But apparently the Pope didn't think we were important enough to be seen.

The hubris.

It's not that one hour a week in Culture Capsule at the Missionary Training Center was useless, mind you. I did learn the words to "The Hunchback Family" in Italian.

Most of my Mormon friends and family returned from their missions to Japan, Finland, Venezuela, Ireland, Belgium, and even Iran with little appreciation for the cultures they'd experienced.

Most of us forgot the languages we'd spoken for two years because there was simply no point in maintaining them. One family member chided me for writing portions of my journal in Italian, quoting a Church leader who'd said it was wrong to "cling" to the language we'd learned on our missions.

I'd say this dismissal of other cultures was a problem particular to Mormons. But it's a problem central to white dominant culture in general. We've been conditioned by hundreds of years of colonialism and presumed superiority to feel no need to consider other points of view.

Mormons face yet another difficulty. We're told not to "delve into the mysteries." We teach the same basic lessons in Sunday School and Priesthood and Relief Society over and over and over. We're never allowed to discuss outside the temple the teachings we learn inside. Even there, we're always watching the same film, hearing the exact same words again and again, allowed only five minutes of meditation—and no discussion—in the Celestial Room.

We're trained from infancy to open our minds only to the bare minimum of information we're told we need. As if one could ever progress to either perfection or godhood with such a limited mindset.

As part of the dominant culture, most white people expect everyone else to learn *our* ways and adapt accordingly. We're unable to see the unlikelihood we could ever achieve perfection without cultivating a competent level of empathy.

I used to feel proud I'd "served" as a missionary. Now I see my time in Italy as cultural imperialism.

Still, I'm glad I went because, despite everything, I did learn something.

I don't like knowing I'm biased. It's painful, annoying, embarrassing. I didn't choose to be biased so it can't be true.

Of course, I didn't choose to be white, either, yet that's also true. I didn't choose to be gay, but it's an undeniable fact. I didn't choose to have hazel eyes.

I didn't choose the local or national culture I grew up in.

It's *hard* to overcome our culture, to be human rather than middle class, to be people rather than Republican or Democrat. It's scary to change our worldview.

As Mormons, we expected it of Roman Catholics in Rome. As Americans, we expect it of other cultures around the world. As white people, we expect it of every other race and ethnicity.

Perhaps other white religious conservatives don't expect to become gods in the afterlife, but many of us act as if we consider ourselves gods right now. Only *we* can be trusted to vote, only *we* deserve due process when encountering the police, only *we* deserve the benefit of the doubt in every situation.

I used to think Mormons were presumptuous to believe they could become gods, even if terrified, irritable, defensive ones. Now I see that same presumption among most white people. We don't need to belong to a white supremacist group to think we're superior, and to act and vote accordingly.

While I'm no longer Mormon, although I no longer believe in any deity, I still have a deeply ingrained desire to be perfect.

Of course, I'm *not*. Neither are any of my white friends and family. Or people of any other race, ethnicity, or religion. But being imperfect doesn't mean we're "bad." Unless we refuse to acknowledge that no matter how much of value we're able to teach others, there will always be plenty we need to learn ourselves.

To whom much is given, much is required.

Did we really expect to "grow" without experiencing pain, self-reflection, and change?

The truth is it's impossible to come anywhere close to being good, much less perfect, if we deny the oppression, suffering, joys, and triumphs of others.

Competence in any field requires practice, and lots of it. If we want to develop cultural competency, if we want to be the best people we can be, here or in the hereafter, we're going to need to start practicing cultural humility more regularly.

So let's rally the courage to make some mistakes, accept our imperfections, and learn how to learn.

Section 2: Policy and Attitude Changes

Perfectionists Against Self-Improvement

“Why are you so mean all the time?” I asked one of the religious conservatives in my life, a Mormon I’d known for years.

“When am I ever mean?” This friend had just posted on social media urging everyone to be Christlike. Immediately afterward, he posted his view that the very concept of institutional racism was evil, and right after that he quoted a leader of the LDS Church wishing everyone joy and peace in their lives.

“Supporting a law absolving people who run over protesters feels a *little* mean,” I ventured. I’d also seen this family member’s post declaring the atrocities committed against Native Americans fully justified. “Locking people in prison for decades over a little cannabis feels mean, too.”

“Enabling someone to sin isn’t compassion,” he countered. “I’m showing tough love. Being hard on people pushes them to better themselves, so I’m doing them a favor. *That’s* compassion.”

“You think being tough on folks who are behaving poorly is a good thing?”

“Don’t you?”

“Why do you think I’m pointing out your poor behavior?”

Another longtime friend, also Mormon, used to share with me words from the language she was creating for the subjects on her future planet. She couldn't be bothered, however, to learn rudimentary Spanish, though thousands of Latinx immigrants lived in her community, some even members of her congregation. Those people were in *America*! It was *their* job to learn a new language, not hers.

One doesn't need to be a polyglot to be a good person, obviously, but it does seem odd that a perfectionist hoping to become a god in the afterlife reached her sixties still disdaining any responsibility on her part to communicate with others of different backgrounds.

While Latter-day Saints may be the only Christians preaching progression to godhood, many other white Christians still seem to feel equally superior to Black and brown neighbors. Indigenous peoples everywhere are treated like bedbug infestations, not as brothers and sisters sharing the same Heavenly parents. It's no more audacious, I suppose, to believe you're on the fast track to deification than to believe God prefers you right here, right now, over someone with a tad more melanin.

Racial bias disguised as sibling rivalry would hardly impress a Being who was truly Supreme, would it? "Dad loves *me* best!"

Even a sinless God wouldn't be able to resist rolling his or her eyes.

I would hope most of us don't *want* to worship a God who treats some humans better than others, who pits his kids against each other like dogs in an illegal dogfight.

A God who is omniscient, omnipresent, and omnipotent surely has enough love to go around. He's not forced to dole it out in zero sum portions.

So why do so many white worshippers keep telling ourselves that we're better? Even flawed sinners who acknowledge they're doomed without God's forgiveness still think they're somehow just a *little* more deserving.

"Ugh, *Just Mercy*? I don't want to watch a movie about Black people in prison."

Our refusal to learn more about others is a deliberate attempt *not* to feel empathy.

Not to feel equal.

We understand that learning would change that dynamic, so we choose not to learn.

I know fellow Mormons who won't watch classic movies like *Train of Life*, *The King's Speech*, or *Precious*. Just as "nothing good happens after midnight," apparently no good can be gleaned from R-rated movies. Ever.

Everybody has their preferences, of course. I get bored with most westerns. But I do watch movies from almost every genre, in at least a dozen different languages. I can't possibly watch every worthwhile movie or television show, read every great book, or listen to every fascinating podcast, but that fact saddens me—it's not an excuse to shrug off my ignorance.

When I saw the first *Highlander* movie and realized the prize for the sole survivor was to experience everything every other person had ever experienced, know everything about the human condition there was to know, I wondered if a Latter-day Saint had written the screenplay. A lapsed one, of course, since the film was rated R. But "the prize" seemed very Mormon.

I was taught that after Judgment Day, everyone would know everything that every single person throughout history had done or felt or thought. This was a necessary step before we could move on to our assigned kingdom. Even folks relegated to the lowest degree of the Telestial Kingdom would intimately understand billions of lives. Those awarded the top level of the Celestial Kingdom, where they'd then continue with their progression toward godhood, would need to learn even more.

To become a god, we'd have to understand everything there was to know about biology, about chemistry and physics and engineering, about music, painting, sculpture, stained glass, and… *everything.*

But when I dare to read the FB posts of my Mormon friends and family, I see them ranting about Critical Race Theory. They call anyone questioning the "kindness" of their favorite slaveowners naïve. They're livid if anyone calls the LDS Church's longtime ban on Black members going to the temple (and thus also qualifying for the Celestial Kingdom and therefore godhood) racist.

They rail against "antifa," though until the last couple of years, they believed that fighting against fascists like Mussolini and Hitler was a good thing.

They love “freedom” and yet blindly follow pundits and politicians who tell them that “undesirables” in our country shouldn’t be allowed to vote.

Everyone has blind spots, and everyone progresses at their own pace.

But that’s really the problem, isn’t it? On so many issues, most of the Mormons I know, and most of the conservative Christians in my circle, think they’ve already reached the pinnacle of enlightenment. There is *no* further advancement to be made. Mormons may still need to learn astronomy before they can become a god, but they’re good in regard to empathy. They’ve nailed that one.

Marked it off the “To Do” list a long time ago.

White Christian evangelicals also seem to know everything they need to understand about poverty, and homelessness, and addiction, and mental health, and immigration, and trans women. They’ve reached the apex of compassion and caring and love.

Which must be why so many of them post memes making fun of gay marriage, Black Lives Matter protesters, and Greta Thunberg.

I may be too intimidated by rock climbing to learn how to do it, but I *want* to. I want to learn architecture and screenwriting and paleontology, too. I want to train for a marathon and learn to play tennis and master the butterfly stroke. In a perfect world, even an Earthly one, I’d learn *everything*.

Shouldn't all of us, religious or not, at the very least want to learn how to be kind to those who are suffering?

As gods in embryo, do my fellow Mormons believe it possible even to become a good, decent person, much less a Supreme Being, by dismissing every other human on the planet who doesn't think and behave exactly like us?

It's not the superior conscience of white Americans telling us to subjugate eighty million non-white Americans.

People lie to themselves all the time about any number of things. But there does finally come a time when we look in the mirror and realize the truth.

My imperfect hope is that we can all push ourselves through the discomfort of real change to understand that any meaningful self-improvement includes doing unto others as we would have them do unto us, *not* doing unto others what we *don't* want done unto us, and just stop being assholes quite so often.

One-Tenth More Empathy to Create Real Change

Most families have a crazy Uncle Bob who ruins holiday gatherings by spouting some racist, sexist, offensive nonsense. As conservative Christians, it's often the other way around—we have a lone family member asking the rest of us to behave more humanely.

Many years have passed since some of my family members have spoken to me. Their abandonment was painful for the longest time, but now when I briefly check their public postings on social media, I couldn't be happier we're no longer in contact.

One recently posted quotes from Mormon prophets and other Latter-day Saint leaders on the need to be Christlike. This was followed almost immediately by a meme comparing Al Bundy (a fictional character) with Oprah Winfrey. Al's financial worth was $2.32 while Oprah's was $2 billion. The meme complained that in the eyes of racial justice advocates, Bundy was supposedly "privileged" while Winfrey was "Oprahssed."

The next post came after Derek Chauvin was convicted for killing George Floyd. "We've GOT to be LOUD and back the BLUE!"

Then came additional posts about the need to be Christlike.

Mormons don't have an Apocrypha but they do have the Joseph Smith Translation of the Bible. Even there, however, there's no Luke 24:12 stating, "Thou shalt allow police officers to kill without accountability, yea, with great impunity."

If Mormons or other evangelical Christians could put even one-tenth of the effort into combatting racism and other forms of injustice that they put into justifying extrajudicial execution, we might have a chance at noticeably reducing oppression in our faith communities and our nation.

What if instead of donating millions to defend a vigilante who killed peaceful demonstrators, we donated funds to buy down medical debt, or establish scholarships, or put solar panels on church roofs?

What if instead of backing "the BLUE"—in all situations, no matter what—we stopped pulling people over for having an air freshener hanging from their rearview mirror? If officers feel mortally threatened during these trivial traffic stops, wouldn't backing the blue mean *not* unnecessarily endangering their lives? Do we really believe our nation will fall into moral decay if we let someone drive around with a black poodle?

Manipulative fundraisers depict the demand to "defund police" as a call for anarchy and pillaging across our communities. When we choose to believe such nonsense instead of hearing the truth, that humane people simply want humane responses to societal problems, we're using our time, our money, our energy—our very lives—to ensure those problems remain unsolved.

With the money local governments spend defending officers or making settlements with the families of victims, we could instead lift our communities in myriad ways. It's financially sound, in addition to being morally appropriate, to treat people fairly.

When I listen to the convoluted reasoning conservative pundits make to justify their racism and then listen to friends and family parrot those reasons, I think, "Couldn't we devote even one-tenth of our energy to empathy? Why not devote one-tenth of our intellectual honesty to learning rather than dismissing? Can't we devote one-tenth of our anger toward demanding justice rather than insisting that those crying for justice be crushed?"

Even those of us who do want to dismantle institutionalized racism often don't devote much effort to doing anything constructive about it. *We* could up our commitment to ten percent as well.

My Mormon friends and family post incessantly about the importance of free will and making good choices and taking responsibility for our actions.

If we could divert one-tenth of our weaponization of those concepts toward choosing to acknowledge and then address bias and discrimination, we might have a chance at making America the moral oasis we seem to think it would be if everyone simply joined our church.

Of course, it's easier to mock and belittle and hate those who point out our failures. It doesn't even bear consideration, apparently, how a white man, even a fictional one, with only $2.32 to his name managed to own a two-story home in the suburbs of Chicago.

So let's rise above simplistic self-righteousness and start devoting at least one-tenth of our humanity toward helping people live better lives. That's so much more Christlike, the Spirit tells me, than wishing them dead.

Oh, Say Can You Unsee?

In fourth grade, I was on first base one afternoon when the next player hit the ball, allowing me to reach second. There, a player on the opposing team told me, "That ball was an out. You have to go back to first."

I slowly walked back while the next player picked up the bat.

And was immediately tagged out.

The guy had *tricked* me!

I was embarrassed for being so gullible, but more than that, I was angry. I'd never been the least bit interested in sports and was making what I felt a Herculean effort to participate, which made the discovery of my ignorance all the more painful.

If I could feel so betrayed by a routine childhood lie, why shouldn't we expect not to experience a far more profound anger at discovering almost everything we've ever been taught about race and slavery isn't accurate? Of *course* we're mad at anyone revealing the truth. It's a classic case of "shooting the messenger."

As a Mormon growing up in New Orleans, I was oblivious to the treatment of Native Americans. When I watched the movie *Billy Jack*, I asked my mom why people were being mean to the Indians. "Aren't they Lamanites?

Don't we like them?" They were the people of the Book of Mormon, after all.

When I learned later of the LDS Church's "Indian Placement Program," in which Native children were placed with white Mormon families, to give them a better chance to assimilate and be "successful" in life, I thought it a great idea. As Mormons, we'd make up for the bad things other white people did to the Indians. I had no knowledge how this fit into a larger history of robbing people of their culture, of Native children forcibly taken and placed with white families, of Native children essentially imprisoned in boarding schools, where they were severely punished if they spoke their native language. I had no idea these children were given new names and forbidden from using their real names. I knew nothing about the long history of whites breaking treaties they'd made with indigenous peoples.

On one of our family vacations, we rode a train around Stone Mountain in Georgia. I took a picture of the "Indian" who rode up alongside us on horseback and pointed a gun at me, my photo looking straight down the barrel of the rifle. A fun game of Cowboys and Indians. On our trip to Wyoming and Montana, we stopped at the site of Custer's Last Stand and learned of the valor of the white men slaughtered by the Indians.

And yet, my family enjoyed repeating that we were pretty sure our paternal grandmother was the descendant of a Cherokee princess. If we squinted and strained real hard, we could almost see indigenous features.

I've learned a bit more since then, no thanks to the schools and universities I attended, no thanks to the film industry, no thanks to my church.

During the prolonged protests and rallies for racial justice in 2020, I learned even more disturbing facts, including the huge number of indigenous women who are murdered or go missing every year. I learned that Black women in the mid-1800s were subjected to brutal medical experiments and surgeries, without anesthesia even when it was available. I learned of the vast number of Black, Latina, and indigenous women who were sterilized, as recently as the 1970s, without their consent.

I learned about Curtis Austin being labeled a felon *just for writing a book* about the Black Panthers. He was not arrested, not tried, not convicted, but still labeled a felon. He didn't even know until his employer called him into the office to discuss his "record."

I learned that some people *did* receive reparations after the Civil War—former slaveowners who were compensated by the government at taxpayer expense for the loss of their human "property."

When I worked in a group home for mentally disabled adults, I saw firsthand the suspicions and prejudices of the neighbors. When a longtime friend went two decades without diagnosis or treatment for her schizophrenia, I saw mass ignorance and fear, even among medical professionals. She went undiagnosed, after all, while working in a hospital.

While I was researching the Upstairs Lounge fire, I learned that it marked the first time in Louisiana history when prison inmates were brought in to collect the bodies because the scene was deemed too gruesome for firefighters or other trained professionals. You know, the good people. There was apparently no concern for the emotional trauma inflicted on prisoners.

When Denny LeBoeuf saw a man crash to the sidewalk from the burning second-floor bar, her boyfriend led her across the street and told her not to watch the horror, that she'd never be able to unsee those images.

Denny went on to work for the ACLU fighting for the rights of prisoners and against capital punishment.

But her boyfriend was right. None of us can pretend we haven't seen the atrocities committed against people of color and other groups.

When I was excommunicated from the Mormon Church, I was called a "son of perdition."

And we've all heard about "gender traitors" and "race traitors."

One of my missionary colleagues recounted a story once about his first semester at Brigham Young University. He and a friend were out walking on campus at night and saw campus security in the distance. Just for the hell of it, they started running and, sure enough, the security officers chased them, automatically assuming the young men must have done something wrong. It was a funny anecdote.

The outcome wasn't as humorous for Byron Lee Williams. When Las Vegas police officers saw him riding his bicycle without a safety light, they began chasing him. He was killed for the three crimes he committed that night: not having a light, fleeing for his life, and being black.

I'm baffled that so many of my Mormon friends and family still refuse to see what's right in front of them.

The thing is… I believe they *do* see it. An LDS friend of mine, married to a woman in the temple, confided in me one day that he was gay. He finally told his bishop some of the things he'd done and was promptly excommunicated, which left him ineligible to attend his daughter's temple wedding. The daughter emailed me, "Don't tell me why he was ex'ed. I don't want to know." But the fact that she said this to *me* meant that she already knew the answer. If the words weren't spoken aloud, though, weren't in writing, weren't communicated to her in any way, she could pretend she didn't know, pretend she was respecting his privacy rather than hiding from the truth.

In the wake of the recent protests against police killings, a prominent Mormon author scoffed at the idea of reparations for the descendants of slaves. Mormons, he pointed out, weren't asking for reparations after being driven from their homes and businesses in Ohio, Missouri, and Illinois. Mormons pulled themselves up by their bootstraps, he explained. He seemed to have missed that the path to this Mormon success story involved invading and confiscating Native American lands, pushing for the enslavement of indigenous people, even killing many of them. And, since he's conveniently forgotten these details, he concludes that we should all just let bygones be bygones.

It's a callousness I'm far too familiar with.

One day, shortly after Ronald Reagan was hospitalized because of an assassination attempt, my mission companion and I were aboard a commuter train just south of Rome. We'd been in Castel Gandolfo on our day off and were now heading back to our apartment in Ciampino.

Suddenly, the train screeched to a halt, and seconds later, the conductor ran past us. My companion grabbed my arm. "Let's go see what's up."

We followed the conductor to the end of the car, where he stared through the glass doors in horror. I turned, saw a stone wall a few feet away, and then noticed an old woman face down in a ditch. She raised her left hand weakly, lowered it, and didn't move again. A spilled bag of groceries lay a few feet away.

The railroad crossing gate was lowered, blocking a small road, and I understood instantly what had happened. The train tracks curved sharply just beyond the road, behind a hill. It was impossible for anyone to have seen the train coming. The woman had probably thought she had plenty of time to cross and didn't want to wait for the train, though it was only a few cars long. She had dinner to prepare.

Other passengers began crowding around us, and the conductor ran to call for help. Outside, I could see a few townspeople from the tiny village starting to gather.

My companion and I could go out there, I thought, and give her a priesthood blessing. We could heal her. We could even raise her from the dead. All it would take was a little faith.

Maybe this was what Italy needed for the work to finally start taking off. My companion and I had only taught two lessons in the past three months, after all. We *needed* a miracle. We could get dozens of people, perhaps hundreds, interested in the Mormon Church if we could muster enough bravery to go out there and bless this woman.

But what if Heavenly Father wouldn't honor any blessing I gave? Just before we'd started back for Ciampino, I'd lusted briefly after a young man playing "Sarà Perché Ti Amo" on the jukebox at a café by Lake Albano. And I remembered that back in Quartu, my previous companion and I had blessed a sick member of the congregation, telling him he'd be healed.

He'd died the following day.

What if we went out there and blessed this woman and nothing happened? It would be mortifying. It might even hurt the missionary effort.

My heart pounding in my chest, I wiped my damp brow and prayed for guidance, for courage. I had to do something before it was too late.

Outside, a few more townspeople were gathering. An old man strolled down with a look of curious bemusement, trying to see what the fuss was all about.

And saw his wife dead in the ditch.

He began wailing and screaming and tearing at his shirt. A few of his neighbors rushed over to comfort him.

The man was still screaming and crying ten minutes later when a bus hired to replace the commuter train came to take passengers the rest of the way to Ciampino and Statuario and Rome.

I remember staring at the weeds along the side of the road as we drove off, wondering if the biggest sin in my life was being gay or if it was looking at this human tragedy only as a tool I could use for my benefit.

Sometimes, we can look at something, *think* we see what's in front of us, and with a slight change of lighting or some other minor shift, suddenly see a completely different reality.

Something similar happened to me years later in August of 2005. My partner had recently died of liver cancer, and I was trying to start my life over again. Because Tom had felt that writing a will would jinx him, his estranged sister was considered next of kin and inherited the life insurance benefit, his pension, the $25K in the bank, the house, and the car.

I'd moved back to an apartment in the Marigny, where the washer and dryer I'd taken with me wouldn't fit through the door.

The bartender at my favorite hangout had died of cancer since I'd moved to the Westbank to live with Tom. One of my favorite fuck buddies, a hairdresser who used to cut my hair in his living room before taking me upstairs to his bed, had died of an overdose.

I didn't even know he used drugs.

I ventured into the Quarter on a Friday evening late in August and ran into another old sex buddy, Mike. He'd been blinded years earlier by cytomegalovirus, long before I first met him, but my own eyes were working fine, and Mike was still a very hot man. I asked if we could spend some time together.

He invited me to his place the upcoming Monday evening to celebrate his birthday.

But I never saw him again.

Because Saturday morning, I learned that a Category 5 hurricane was heading for New Orleans. I grabbed a change of clothes, my meds, my passport, birth certificate, and resumé, and got out of town.

I never saw my apartment again, either.

There were countless calls to "Rebuild!" in the aftermath, but I now saw New Orleans differently. I remembered my first flood. And my second. And my third and my fourth.

I remembered being with my second partner and hearing heavy rain one evening and then worriedly looking out the door. "That's a flooding rain," I told him, already familiar with the sound. But everything seemed OK.

A half hour later when we turned on the evening news, a reporter announced "massive flooding all across the city."

I ran back to the door, discovering my car already under water. Worse, the water was still rising and soon spilled over the threshold.

Just as the electricity went out.

My partner and I tried picking things off the floor by candlelight as the dirty water continued to rise. We had to save our ferrets. We had to save my schoolbooks. I had a final exam at 8:00 the next morning.

We received fourteen inches of rain in two hours. And it was just another spring storm, not even a hurricane.

Living in New Orleans after Katrina was not sustainable. This kind of disaster was going to happen again. And again.

As soon as the computers came back up in the city I'd evacuated to, I bought a ticket for Seattle to start anew with my one suitcase of belongings.

As missionaries, we were taught to focus on (i.e., target) folks who'd just gone through some type of psychological upheaval. They'd be more prepared to feel the Spirit (i.e., more vulnerable to emotional manipulation).

The thing is, it's true that those whose lives are shattered often gain new perspective.

Here in Seattle, I've grown used to summer air so thick with smoke from wildfires I can't see to the end of the block. I'd already purchased a supply of masks long before the pandemic began.

I can't unsee climate change.

I can't unsee the damage cruel theology and self-serving religious policies inflict.

And I can't unsee racism.

I used to feel proud I'd served as a missionary. Then I began to feel embarrassed I had the audacity to tell Christians in Rome they had to join the "true" church. Now I tell people I worked as a door-to-door salesman for two years.

I'd sung or heard "The Star-Spangled Banner" for several decades before I read the third verse, with the lyrics, "No refuge could save the hireling and slave from the terror of flight or the gloom of the grave." Patriotic Americans feel robbed of their anthem when these words are pointed out. But the words have been there all along. We just weren't told about them. Once heard, though, they can't be unheard.

That's not the messenger's fault.

Oppressors use the gay panic defense whenever they can. They use the black panic defense and the protester panic defense. There seems to be a homeless panic defense and poverty panic defense as well. Even a freedom panic defense.

It's odd that many who call the order to wear masks during a pandemic an infringement on their rights have little problem with a secret, unidentified police/military force kidnapping non-violent protesters off the streets, throwing them into unmarked vans, and whisking them away to unknown destinations.

I suppose there's a hierarchy among panic defenses, and the one regarding *other* citizens losing their freedom isn't very close to the top.

More and more of us have finally seen the truth. It's painful and it's embarrassing. And more than a little sad. But isn't it better to stop believing things that aren't true?

Exposure Isn't Enough

We frequently hear stories of parents who were rabid homophobes… until one of their own children turns out to be gay. We hear about Christians who believe stereotypes about Jews… until they meet someone at work who is Jewish. We even hear, less frequently, about white supremacists who begin interacting with Black people and finally see the light.

But not all parents of LGBTQ kids become advocates. Not all religious bigots learn to love their neighbors as themselves. And for sure not every biased person overcomes bias simply by working alongside someone of a different race or ethnicity.

Men have been living and working with women for decades without fully acknowledging the problems of unequal pay, sexual harassment, and lack of promotion.

We see poverty every day. We step right over homeless people. We're able to ignore their suffering because we don't understand the forces that have created it. And we're unable to do anything to combat the misery of millions all around us unless we understand.

Clearly, proximity alone isn't going to do the job. Exposure to others who are unlike us isn't enough. That exposure must be coupled with education.

A white man, I taught at a Black university for ten years and managed to learn almost nothing about systemic racism. Every administrator I worked with was black. 95% of my students in every class for ten years was black. But I didn't understand the problems I saw all about me. I had no context for them, no framework in which to put the pieces I grasped here and there. Instead, I saw things only through the lens of my white, suburban upbringing.

I was able to work in this predominantly Black environment for a full decade without lessening my biases, without even recognizing them. If anything, my biases grew stronger because I misinterpreted so much of what I did see.

Such a lost opportunity.

In a perfect world, everyone would be self-motivated to do all the research necessary to learn about every form of injustice in our society and in other societies across the planet. But that's simply not realistic. Most of us can't even muster the energy to Google something. If we aren't provided a link, we simply don't bother looking it up.

Guilting our friends and family—or ourselves—for not taking a little more initiative might feel good, might feel bad, but either way, it's ineffective.

So what *can* we do?

Since bias is a problem at every level of our culture, we must address it in as many different institutions as possible.

First, we set aside a couple of hours each week for ourselves, perhaps Saturday morning, maybe Thursday evening, whatever works, and dedicate that time to watching a film, listening to a podcast, or reading an article or book. Perhaps we stream a relevant video while riding our stationary bike. Maybe we listen to a podcast during our daily walk.

If the time isn't set aside, we'll keep postponing this essential education. To make sure we don't get bogged down looking for something to read without ever getting to the actual reading, we can start by looking up a beginner's list of resources. They're all over the internet.

We can also try some of this as a couple or as a family.

It's possible this will be as much as we can control, but we might try to get similar programs going in our local religious organizations.

We can ask HR at work if our employer can offer trainings on bias. If they offer none, then establishing one is a step forward. If they already offer three, adding a fourth is an achievable goal.

We can push for local school boards to include bias training not only for the teachers and staff but for students as well.

A semester or two of bias training at the college level should be a prerequisite for graduation with *any* degree because without it we're not fully preparing college grads for the workplace.

We need to find individual ways to incorporate bias training in everything we do. We belong to a quilting club with mostly white members? Let's find books or documentaries on African American quilting and share them with the group.

We host a website on gardening? Let's add a tab with links to YouTube channels featuring Black gardeners and include a list of additional resources on bias, even if they have nothing specifically to do with gardening. We can do the same if our website is about model airplanes or if we're advertising our construction company. And if we have no website, we can add a link or two to our email signature line for every email we send out.

If we're to combat racism, or sexism, or ableism, or any other kind of bias throughout our society, we need to address it *everywhere.*

Even making it easier for people won't guarantee that they'll click on the links provided, watch the movies suggested, read even a single article. But we'll make it *more* likely.

And just as importantly, we make sure that no one can glide through life ignoring the problems altogether. Universal healthcare was a fringe idea (in the U.S.) until Bernie Sanders ran for president. We still haven't implemented it, but now we talk about it almost daily. Driving an idea into the consciousness of more people is an important step toward accomplishing any social change.

It's why representation matters in film and on television. The first interracial couples on TV were scandalous. Now no one blinks an eye. A perfume commercial shows two women in love? Sure, some people still wail about the end of humanity, but more and more people just see it as normal. Because it is.

To succeed, bias training must become normalized in as many places as possible. Most of us have already started educating ourselves, and we can try now to begin making it easier for the others we work, worship, and share family dinners with.

It will almost certainly be uncomfortable at first, but the truth is we know too much now to ever go back to blissful ignorance.

Mandatory Courses on Race, Gender, and Social Justice

Every degree from every accredited college, university, or trade school must include at least one mandatory course on race, gender, and social justice. There is no field in which students and workers do not need to understand the history of discrimination and the ways oppression still occurs in virtually every work environment in America.

I grew up in New Orleans, with extended family in rural Mississippi. As a child, I was given Confederate caps and flags to play with. When we visited Vicksburg, my mother told me, "Oh, don't look at *that* monument. It's for Yankees. Ooh! Look at *this* monument! It's for *us*!"

I also grew up Mormon, in my late teens before the LDS Church "allowed" Blacks to hold the priesthood. Women still can't.

Serving as a full-time volunteer missionary in Naples, I was forbidden from visiting Pompeii. Our mission president said we'd be too tempted to sin if we saw any of the scandalous murals or other artwork.

Even when many of us have had extraordinary opportunities, they've often been deliberately snatched from our grasp.

As a gay man whose personal politics grew increasingly progressive throughout my adulthood, I am still woefully ignorant of the history of oppression and of ways to diminish institutional racism and sexism and all the other types of discrimination which occur throughout society.

I earned one Biology and three English degrees. While literature helped me understand other cultures and social classes a bit more, there was never any instruction specifically on race and gender. I had to pick up little snippets here and there. I also taught at a Black university for ten years. An eye-opening experience, I still only caught brief glimpses of my unintentional but still harmful bias and discriminatory behavior.

Random learning isn't sufficient.

I found myself shocked by the racism and sexism I witnessed among some of my gay friends in New Orleans, disturbed that so many people seemed unable to transform their own suffering into understanding the suffering of others.

After relocating to liberal Seattle in the wake of Hurricane Katrina, a disaster which itself taught me more about racism, I married another ex-Mormon who believed in social justice. My husband became involved in Socialist politics, and I volunteered with Radical Women. But because my work schedule didn't allow me time to take actual coursework, I still only learned bits and pieces.

I recently watched *Hidden Figures*, horrified to witness a scientist who wasn't allowed to use the bathroom in her building. Instead, she had to run half a mile, in heels, sometimes in the rain, every time she needed to pee. How did I not already know about this demeaning, humiliating, everyday oppression?

My current employer feels it important to address racial and social justice. Every employee is required to participate in an annual all-day training. I also chose to take three additional half-day trainings—Implicit Bias I, Implicit Bias II, and Internalized Racial Superiority. I was astonished to learn that the Irish were not considered white during part of American history, that Finnish people weren't considered white, either. It reinforced my understanding of race as a social construct, but I realized immediately I needed an entire semester of such instruction, at the very least. If I had reached the age of 57 without knowing these basic facts, how much more history did I, a reasonably well-educated adult, not know?

A Black co-worker asked me why I was taking this training. "Because I don't want to be an asshole," I replied. "Or at least be less of one."

Yes, we could all study on our own, but the realities of life too often prevent that from happening, even for people who want to learn. And it's just as important, perhaps more so, that people who aren't interested in learning about these issues do so anyway.

Something so essential to the success and security of our nation can't be left to chance, any more than we would allow citizens to choose whether or not they felt personally compelled to pay their income tax, or to get a driver's license before sitting behind the wheel of a car.

If our country is ever going to be truly post-racial, ever truly cease its misogyny and finally treat all people equally regardless of color, gender, orientation, religion, or anything else, then everyone must learn about these issues, much earlier and more fully than I have. Some of this history should be introduced in middle school and high school, and then taught in even more depth in every accredited institution of higher learning. People in every field of study or work must understand oppression and ways to reduce our complicity in continuing it.

Mandatory courses on race, gender, and social justice should be prerequisites for graduation into society because everyone, even those already enjoying privilege, will benefit both financially and emotionally once all people are treated with equal respect, humanity, and justice.

Church Courses to Overcome Unconscious Bias

If we're not prejudiced, why do we resist anti-racist behaviors and policies so strenuously? Most of the white Mormons in my life are in fact *anti*-anti-racist.

I finally understand now how Anti-Nephi-Lehies must have felt.

Fortunately, more conservative white Christians are finally coming to understand that if we don't have a prejudiced bone in our body, we should *want* to help alleviate the oppression of others.

After all, Pontius Pilate didn't truly absolve himself of all responsibility simply by washing his hands.

It's one thing for us to control our personal behavior. Not being the racist who shoots Latinx shoppers or the guy who runs over a Black jogger is undoubtedly a good thing. But there are far more ways to inflict harm than by picking up a weapon.

And controlling our own behavior is far too limited a response. We must also step up and be a force challenging racism is each institution we're part of—local and federal government, the workplace, and even religion.

Uncle Jeff made a disparaging comment about Asians at a family gathering? For many people of all faiths, family is the most important institution in our lives. To protect it, we must call out inappropriate behavior whenever we see it. Gently, if possible. More firmly if necessary.

For Latter-day Saints, the Church is the second-most important institution. Many Mormons, in fact, despite claims that family is their top priority, clearly put religion first.

But does this mean that LDS leaders, past or present, get a pass on *everything*?

How about everyday members of our congregations? When a friend of mine was called to serve a mission in Portland, Oregon, she was thrilled. "Mt. St. Helens just blew up," she said happily. "Heavenly Father is preparing people for the missionaries."

When an earthquake struck Irpinia during my mission, killing 3000 people, the missionaries were excited there, too. We were sure this was God helping us. People who were suffering were more open to hearing the gospel.

Why did none of our friends and family call us out for such horrific comments?

If our husband has an affair, he's excommunicated until he repents and is rebaptized. If Mom becomes an alcoholic, we arrange an intervention and try to help her into rehab.

We have no problem accepting—or demanding—consequences for family members. So why can't we expect appropriate behavior from Church leaders?

Even if we suspect a leader has received the Second Anointing, it doesn't mean he *can't* sin.

Every human being has moral failings. If we don't want to face renaming our buildings and institutions again and again each time society makes additional moral advancements, we should consider not naming anything at all after flawed people. What's wrong with Zion University? Deseret University?

If the Liahona was a compass helping the faithful move in the right direction, why not Liahona University? What's wrong with Eternal Progress University or Millennium University or even plain old Mormon University?

Oh, wait, we can't say Mormon anymore.

So it appears we *can* change *some* names. Excellent. Then why not this one?

Most Mormons, even most BYU students, have no idea who J. Reuben Clark was. Few people are going to spend three days at home crying inconsolably if we change the name of the BYU Law School. Again, we're not obliged to place the name of a different morally compromised individual on the building. Why not something like Secular Human Law School? That's what's being taught there, isn't it? Or we could go in exactly the opposite direction. When I served as a Mormon missionary in Italy, I was surprised to see a financial institution named Banco di Santo Spirito. I suppose BYU could have a Law School of the Holy Ghost. If these aren't entirely satisfying names, we can draw committees to discuss other options, perhaps assign law students to come up with lists of possibilities, determine the winner through a debate or mock trial.

Which commandment, specifically, do we think we're breaking by changing the name of a university?

A single act, of course, won't "solve" racism in our communities. We'll need to make a far more concerted effort.

In the Missionary Training Center, we spent one hour each week in Culture Capsule. Some of the stuff we learned was nonsense, but forty years later, I can still sing "Volare" and "Santa Lucia" and "Bella Ciao." We can easily develop a similar learning program at church. If we don't feel like replacing an existing hour or adding another, we can at least establish a separate weekly fireside.

Or perhaps we could implement a type of home study program. I graduated from Seminary without ever attending early morning classes. In my stake, we had home study. We could likewise provide weekly assignments to help uncover our biases—a specific film, podcast, or article—and then hold a discussion.

People of other faiths can make similar adaptations to their worship and study programs.

If we need to hear about faith once a week, tithing twice a week, prayer three times a week, and repentance four times a week, we certainly need to hear about bias and equity and racial justice more than once a year.

There's no need, though, to make this solely about race. Most of us would benefit from understanding a bit more about the obstacles facing folks with various disabilities, mental health issues, or any other difference mainstream society uses, intentionally or not, to marginalize others.

My husband and I enjoy School Night once a week, our own version of Family Home Evening, where we watch a documentary that teaches us more about historically oppressed groups. If LDS leaders consider Church members part of their gospel family, they should want to help us all grow into stronger anti-racists.

As members of a community larger than ourselves, we can work together to understand our spiritual brothers and sisters, even if they're not exactly like us, even if individual Mormon leaders or Church doctrines bear no responsibility for a particular form of exclusion.

Making ourselves, our families, and our society better can't stop merely with our personal behavior. We must also be a blessing to our families, our local communities, and to our nation.

We can only do that, of course, if declaring "Well, *I'm* not prejudiced" isn't the beginning and end of our efforts.

Subsidizing Cultural Appreciation

The government, as an act of national security, must offer incentives, tax breaks, and subsidies to encourage all businesses and communities to bridge the cultural divides of its people.

Our country is being torn apart by these cultural differences. Parents disown their children, children disown their parents, and lifelong friendships crumble beneath the constant onslaught of hateful rhetoric. People lash out against total strangers. Public figures encourage their supporters to violence. America has experienced this before, and we are fast approaching a moment when one more gunshot or cruel lie can set in motion another massive round of misery, death, and property loss.

Governments routinely assist industries that might fail without their help, companies or corporations whose collapse would negatively impact the entire nation. We subsidize farmers, we bail out banks and auto manufacturers. We even give billions of dollars in tax breaks to fossil fuel corporations already making record profits just to make doubly and triply sure they're financially sound. If we can do all that, we can surely invest the funds necessary to reduce the violence, discord, and gridlock we face when we consistently fail to get through to each other at home and work.

Just as teachers are required to enroll in Continuing Education courses to keep their teaching certificates, employees in every field can be required to attend bias training in the workplace on a regular basis. Employers and community centers can also offer Movie Nights, Book Clubs, and Music Appreciation Hours where different cultures are explored at each meeting. Community colleges and universities can offer subsidized courses to help us understand differences in religion and ethnicity and nationality and physical ability.

I grew up in a white, middle-class suburb. Everyone in my family used the N-word routinely. As a child, I wasn't even allowed to watch shows with black characters. When I was "called" to volunteer two years as a Mormon missionary in Rome, I stuck a pin on a map of the world in the foyer of our congregation alongside the pins of the other missionaries serving from our stake. Sometimes, members milling about would try to guess where the missionaries had been sent, not quite able to tell despite the national outlines on the map.

And I was as ignorant as everyone else.

Fortunately, being exposed to various cultures in Italy changed my life forever. I didn't "convert" many Italians, but I learned how to be part of a global community. I interacted with people living in abject poverty. I worked with illiterate adults, people who'd been involved in organized crime, with gypsies, with highly educated and generous people. I worked with refugees and immigrants from Romania, Ghana, and numerous other countries.

It was impossible not to see the world differently after that.

Upon returning to the U.S., I studied Spanish, French, Russian, Hebrew, and American Sign Language. I taught for ten years at a historically Black university.

And I *still* had trouble getting rid of many of the harmful biases ingrained in me from infancy, that are still being ingrained in me by the dominant culture even now.

Helping millions of Americans understand that all people deserve respect will be a task requiring enormous funding and many years of dedicated effort.

But the alternative is to become another Yugoslavia descending into a bloody civil war leaving it split into tiny pieces, to become a European Union before it was united, with its centuries of acrimony and warfare.

Officials at all levels of government—city, county, state, and federal—must recognize the existential threat of *not* addressing the cultural divides in every corner of our nation. We aren't required to *like* the differences we see, but if we don't understand them, we'll continue to be manipulated by unscrupulous leaders who vilify others for political gain.

When I worked at a credit union, one day a year we closed to the public, and every employee was required to "volunteer" with a local charity. Most of us simply don't have the time to work in food banks or sort through donated clothing. So our credit union paid us to do it. Even if we were unhappy about the chores assigned to us, we learned something about poor, sick, or otherwise disadvantaged people in our community.

This is the approach we need to take as a nation, only we must engage in these activities more than eight hours a year. It's an investment in community, crime reduction, peace, and, yes, productivity. Our taxes already pay for public education, for fire departments, for police departments, for libraries, for parks, and for museums. The need for a populace whose individual components don't constantly want to kill or imprison or oppress each other in whatever way possible is the difference between singing "The Rotten Bones Are Trembling" and "I'm Proud To Be An American."

We can pay people to learn second and third languages. A multilingual workforce can better serve the variety of Americans already here and can compete more effectively in a global economy.

I did not lose anything by learning more about other languages, cultures, and religions. I'm still me, I'm still American, and I'm more committed than ever to champion justice and equality, to support others who are much better champions. We'll never be experts on every culture and religion and ethnicity, but we need a working knowledge if we are to survive as a nation, and we do not have anything close to minimal competency now.

Investing in a lifelong program to educate Americans about other Americans is not only morally and socially worthwhile, but essential for economic and political stability as well.

Deadnaming our Military Bases

When I researched my book on the Upstairs Lounge fire, one of the survivors I interviewed was a trans woman. I was including childhood stories of the people involved in the fire to help readers see that these were real human beings, not statistics. But the trans woman wouldn't tell me her birth name. I was confused. Wasn't that former person still her? Weren't the first twenty years of her life still part of her history? I'm sorry to say that I had no concept of "deadnaming" at the time. Perhaps it's the worst analogy possible to advance racial justice, since so many folks who are insensitive to the continuing damage caused by racist naming are those least likely to respect transgender rights. But those of us who do want to right wrongs must stop deadnaming our military bases by honoring Civil War leaders and white supremacists.

We're resistant to name change in general. Some towns in England still bear Celtic names dating back over 2500 years, even though few residents know what the names mean anymore. For decades after St. Petersburg in Russia was renamed Petrograd, folks would often include the previous name when discussing the city: "Petrograd, formerly St. Petersburg,…" And as soon as the Soviet Union was dissolved, the name of the city quickly reverted.

In the early 19th century, members of The Church of Jesus Christ of Latter-day Saints hated being called Mormons. But the name persisted, and eventually, both

Church leaders and the membership embraced it. There was even an official "I'm a Mormon!" campaign spearheaded by the Prophet and twelve apostles, along with a Church-sponsored video, *Meet the Mormons*. And then, without warning, a later president of the Church declared "Mormon" a slur and demanded an immediate transition to the "proper" name. Not even "Latter-day Saint" was appropriate any longer. The only acceptable term was "members of The Church of Jesus Christ of Latter-day Saints." And the T in "The" had to be capitalized.

It was a mouthful, and most people, even members themselves, refused to adapt. Others, who for years had gladly embraced the name Mormon, now suddenly started calling people out, saying the "M-word" was every bit as offensive as the N-word. Still, weeks and even months passed before the official Church website, Mormon.org, changed its name and the Mormon Tabernacle Choir was renamed Tabernacle Choir on Temple Square.

Many of us remember the tedious way we had to refer to "the artist formerly known as Prince." Some Hispanics want to be called Latinx. Some want to be called Hispanic. Some African Americans want to be called black. Some want the B capitalized and some don't. Some black people want to be called African American. It used to be OK to say "colored." Now it's not. But it is OK to say "people of color."

Naming military bases after Confederates and white supremacists isn't about semantics. It's not about political correctness. These bases weren't named *before* the Civil

War. People aren't resistant to changing the names just because they're used to them. They're not opposed because they want to "remember" history. There's little chance folks in the south are going to forget the Civil War anytime soon. The "honor" of the Confederacy was drilled into me for years by my family in Mississippi.

White people aren't refusing to remove statues honoring traitors because they're committed history buffs who value education above all else. We can learn what we need to know about the Confederacy and Civil War from books, classes, museums, and documentaries. The reason so many white folks don't want to stop deadnaming military bases is because they can't accept that there is no justification for racism—they don't *want* racism to be dead.

The young trans woman I interviewed who'd lost her partner in the Upstairs Lounge fire continued to set out his clothes every morning for weeks, knowing that if she stopped, she'd have to accept the reality he wasn't coming back.

There was immediate white outrage when a Confederate statue in Raleigh was "lynched," a piece of metal that was never alive. Yet many of these same folks refuse to acknowledge the long history of lynching non-white Americans. "Good" people don't insist on idolizing statues of those who promoted a system of inhumanity and murder. "Good" people find ways to celebrate the good things in their culture, not the bad.

Valiant opposition to renaming our military bases after heroes on the *right* side of history is a continual endorsement of treason. If our feelings are hurt because we can no longer openly praise those who fought *against* the U.S., perhaps we're yelling, "Go back to your country!" at the wrong folks. Americans who love America must not only "allow" but also *insist* we rename our military bases.

When Protesting Genocide Is a Racist Act

Some of my Mormon friends and relatives post frequently about the atrocity of racial genocide. But, like many white conservatives of the religious right, the only racial injustice they seem able to detect anywhere in the world is that heaped upon whites by people of color.

My friends and relatives sound the alarm regularly about blacks killing whites, recently posting a photo of several black Africans in South Africa marching with white baby dolls nailed to posts, quite a horrifying image.

Still, I admit to feeling ambivalent about their repeated calls for justice. It's like a police officer ticketing a black driver for speeding. Yes, the driver was breaking the law, but when it's almost exclusively black drivers who get ticketed in a given county or principality, while white drivers speed on by, the enforcement of a law we all agree is good becomes a racist act, not the embodiment of justice.

My Mormon friends and relatives, like so many other conservatives, don't protest when white police officers kill unarmed blacks. I don't hear a word from them about the multiple documented cases of voter suppression, when ballots collected from black voters are discarded, or polling places in majority black areas are eliminated. My conservative Mormon friends and family don't protest against President Trump's Muslim ban, or about Israeli atrocities against Palestinians. I don't hear a word in support of desperate immigrants and refugees trying to enter the Promised Land.

But if a white person anywhere in the world is hurt or killed by non-whites, *that's* worth talking about.

And it *is*.

But when they don't talk about oppression and violence against whites when it is perpetrated by other whites, I can't quite believe their sense of outrage isn't tinged with racism. I don't hear my conservative Mormon friends and relatives protesting Wal-Mart's low wages forcing thousands of its white employees to apply for food stamps and other government assistance.

I don't hear any complaints about a for-profit healthcare system that refuses care to millions of white people, leading to tens of thousands of premature white deaths every year. I hear nothing when a white domestic terrorist kills dozens of whites at a country music concert, a single act which killed more whites than all the white farmers killed in South Africa last year.

But liberals and progressives are awful because they don't care about white genocide in South Africa!

Yes, we do care about the murder of white people. It's just not the *only* thing we care about. We care that even after the end of apartheid, South Africa remains a nation with perhaps the most extreme income inequality in the world.

Closer to home, we care about conservatives removing elected officials in Flint, Michigan and poisoning its water supply. We care that, years later, the problem still hasn't been resolved. I haven't heard any of my religious conservative relatives say a word in support of reparations for the descendants of African slaves. I haven't heard them say anything *against* reparations, either. The issue seems completely unimportant to them.

That's a problem.

If the only injustices my right-wing friends and family care about are those which afford them the opportunity to demonize blacks or other people of color, it's difficult not to see their protests against genocide as a racist act. Especially when they offer no suggestions for how to resolve the racial problems in South Africa or anywhere else. The point of the posts I see is simply that blacks are bad and white people are the real victims in today's world of political correctness.

We don't need to compete for whose injuries are worse. We should be able to unite and together fight injustice everywhere we see it. We on the left are willing to side with conservatives when they are oppressed, with whites when they are oppressed, with anyone anywhere who is oppressed. But to be successful, we're going to need religious conservatives to care about justice for more than just themselves.

Let's work together to make the world a safer place for everyone.

That Time I Wasn't Killed by the Police

If I was black, piercing my nipple might have gotten me killed. It was the day after Angel pushed a needle through my right nipple in her French Quarter salon and slipped a surgical steel ring through it when I made a potentially fatal error while crossing Esplanade Avenue. I hadn't come to a complete stop in the median before crossing the far lane into the Marigny. A second later, I saw a flashing light, groaned, and pulled over.

My first thought was how to appear non-threatening. I'd been turned down for an appearance in *Miller's Crossing* because I looked too gentle for the gangster movie. ("Oh, no!" the casting director exclaimed when she saw me. "Oh, dear no!")

But I'd discovered after coming out that a newfound confidence in my bearing seemed to worry people. If I was walking along the sidewalk and a car stopped beside me at a light, I could hear the quick thump-thump-thump-thump as the driver quickly locked all the doors. Once, after visiting my father in Metairie, I watched as a man in a pickup truck eyed me carefully when I left the house. He circled the block two more times, still eying me. Was he cruising me way out here in the suburbs? But no, he thought I looked "shady" and so on his third lap around the block stopped to knock on my father's door and "warn" him about me. I felt a bit proud of myself.

Still, a police officer thinking I was suspicious was another matter. I figured if I stayed in the car, he wouldn't be able to see whether or not I had a weapon on the seat beside me. Perhaps he'd worry I had a gun in the glove compartment. I'd be less threatening, I decided, standing outside the car where he could tell at a glance I was empty handed. So I exited the vehicle.

That turned out not to be the desired behavior.

I followed the officer's order to get back inside. He cautiously approached the window a moment later. "You didn't come to a full stop," he informed me. "And you weren't wearing a seat belt."

I had tried to put on my seat belt earlier, but the shoulder strap ran directly over my sore nipple. It was still bleeding a day after the piercing, and despite meticulous care for the following six months, it would never heal, so I eventually removed the ring. But that day, since my car had two separate belts, one crossing my waist and the other my chest, I'd decided to wear just the lower one. While I was developing an interest in the leather community, I was *not* into S&M.

Fortunately, my explanation came across as sincere, not confrontational. The officer verified that my belts did come in two straps and let me go with a ticket only for the stop sign violation.

I was aware things could have gone much worse, but I didn't understand just how much worse for many years. I'd had few encounters with the police by that point, have had only a handful more since. I'd been given a speeding ticket once for going twenty-five in a school zone, though I'd gone below the speed limit until the last five feet of the zone, speeding up just a moment too soon. I'd also been issued a ticket for running a red light, when in reality I'd noticed the light turning yellow right as I passed beneath it, after I'd already entered the intersection. So I knew that police officers could stretch the truth or exploit technicalities to make their quota.

But interactions with the police had never been more than an occasional annoyance. And even if I was irritated during a couple of these encounters, I would never have dared to behave rudely. I'd been voted Most Courteous in high school. I'd been a Sunday School teacher for years. I was the guy who crossed the street when I saw a crow looking for food on the sidewalk. One of us had to move—why shouldn't it be me?

I was probably lucky never to be ticketed for jaywalking.

Perhaps a year after my nipple piercing, when my car broke down one time too many, I gave up driving and switched to public transportation. The bus was a hassle, but I knew almost immediately I was never going back to driving. My father, though, surprised me with a used car. It was quite generous of him, even if I didn't recognize at the time our privilege allowing the transfer of capital from one generation to the next. I thanked him for the unexpected gift, but I never drove that car even once. It sat parked along the curb in front of my apartment for another year.

Once, an accident on the corner resulted in a paint can flying off the back of a truck onto my car, spilling white paint across the trunk. It would be too embarrassing to be seen in the vehicle now, but when my annual brake tags expired, I decided I'd better at least drive to the Shell station on Esplanade and get them renewed. I soon discovered, though, that a car left idle for so many months no longer had a functioning battery. One of these days, I'd have to do something about it, but immediate action wasn't necessary. I'd have sold the car long before except I didn't want my father to feel offended.

Then one day, I came home and discovered the car missing. My first thought was that the City had towed it for being abandoned. Good riddance. I wouldn't have to worry about the damn thing anymore.

The following day, I called the impound to verify and discovered the car *hadn't* been towed, so I called the police to report it stolen.

Two officers came to my apartment. "Why did you wait so long to report this?"

"I didn't think anyone would bother jumping a dead battery to steal it."

"Uh huh."

"And I don't need you to look for the car. My insurance only covers liability, not replacement, and I don't want it back. I just thought I ought to document the theft so it would be on record."

"Uh huh."

It would be years before I understood that any one of these incidents could have developed much differently if I weren't white. Even now, I realize my primary motivation for easing the officer's worry when I was stopped on Esplanade was to make *his* day better, not mine. I knew the worst that might happen to me was being slapped with a fine, one I deserved for my transgression. I was trying to spare *the officer* a bad encounter.

Behaving in a civil, polite manner is a good thing, but I find the amount of privilege necessary for me to hold such a mindset rather mind-boggling now.

The other day, I saw that Homeland Security Secretary Chad Wolf promised to send armed federal agents to Portland and other cities across the country to make "proactive" arrests, *a la* the dystopian world of *Minority Report.* I saw Portland's mayor tear gassed, saw Trump gloating about it.

When I kissed my husband goodnight before bed, he squeezed my hand. "I'm a Trotsky Socialist," he said. "When the 'secret police' take me some time in the next few months before the election, I want you to remember I love you."

It's the closest I've ever come to having "the talk" that many black kids get from their parents by the time they reach middle school. And my husband and I are no longer even middle-aged.

Hopefully, nothing "bad" will happen to me or my loved ones directly. Lots of kids who get "the talk" escape the worst in their personal lives. But far too many don't.

And I'm really not sure how to balance realism and gaslighting and optimism and the suspicion I'm witnessing the Fall of the Roman Empire.

So I'm unclear just how much longer my privilege will last. But while I still have it, I'll try to use that privilege to push forward solutions to many of our most pressing problems, including work to dismantle the structural racism that gave me that privilege in the first place.

Things to Say to Police While Being Murdered

The white governor of a small Mississippi town dismissed George Floyd's claim that he was being suffocated. "If you can say you can't breathe, you're breathing." We heard the same thing when Eric Garner was choked to death for the violent crime of selling loose cigarettes. Technically, the claim is true. A person does need some degree of air flow to be able to speak. But is it fair to expect someone facing imminent death to be 100% scientifically accurate? "Officer, I believe you are increasingly obstructing my air flow by 14.2 percent every 33 seconds, and at this rate, my red blood cells will be unable to provide oxygen for my brain within the next minute and 48 seconds. Give or take ten seconds. I'm afraid I left my oximeter at home."

Since police officers are unwilling to accept "I can't breathe!" as a motivation to stop their assault on an unarmed suspect, perhaps we can come up with a list of better options for those of us being killed.

"You're killing me!"

I'm not sure that expression would work, though, despite its simplicity. I keep hearing my mother's voice. "Stop crying or I'll really give you something to cry about!" And we need to avoid exclamation points. Police officers don't like suspects with attitude.

How about, "I have an underlying medical condition that your assault is aggravating. I may stop breathing or go into cardiac arrest if you don't desist."

OK, we're back to that "I can't breathe!" awkwardness again.

Perhaps a gentle reminder? "Writing a bad check doesn't carry the death penalty, even if a jury of my peers does decide I'm guilty, *after* a trial, *and* a conviction."

People who are being killed should also keep in mind other phrases we can substitute into this template: "going five miles over the speed limit," "being a scofflaw," "hanging out with friends." We can laminate a card with this information and carry it around in our wallets, review it during quiet moments so we'll be able to recall the necessary phrases for specific occasions.

We can even role play with our loved ones. The family that practices being murdered together stays together.

Another option is to wear a T-shirt every time we step out of the house—even if everyone else at our workplace wears business attire—with one helpful phrase on the front and another on the back. We can include the alerts in two or three languages to recognize the multi-cultural make-up of our police force. Light-skinned folks might consider easily readable tattoos on their arms, their necks, even their heads if they're the type who like shaving off their hair or have managed to reach the age when they naturally start to go bald.

Obviously, the safest course of action is to *never* commit any infraction of any kind ever, under any circumstances. We might stand a better chance of not being choked to death, but if we hope to protect ourselves against other forms of killing, we still need to come up with another set of phrases we can shout out at a moment's notice. When we're asleep in bed and police officers shoot us eight times in the middle of the night, we don't have a lot of time to explain that drug possession is another of those crimes that doesn't carry the death penalty. It's an especially difficult sentence to blurt out since we don't even know why we're being shot. Or who the police are looking for. Or that they're even police in the first place. What phrase are we supposed to use? Just start making random guesses?

A friend did try a sign on his front lawn once that read, "You've got the wrong house," but then the mail carrier stopped delivering his mail.

He placed a different sign on his bedroom door, using luminescent ink. "There might be someone in here you're not expecting." And then his girlfriend dumped him.

These things get so complicated. Maybe we should do a study. Come up with a task force.

Perhaps we could purchase some kind of surgically-implanted device that would automatically shout out the appropriate alerts to the police officers killing us without *our* needing to say anything at all. The offending officer might be more open to criticism if it wasn't coming directly from us.

I'm sure we'll come up with a workable solution eventually. We can't be expected to come up with a good answer right on the spot.

After all, it's not as if we've known about this problem for more than a month or so.

Or a year. Or twenty years. Or fifty. Or four hundred.

Ban All Routine Traffic Stops

Dismantling institutional racism can't be completed overnight, but we *can* take steps to begin breaking off critical pieces right away. One easy yet essential advance is to ban traffic stops that don't involve immediate threats to public safety.

We've all seen police engage in high-speed car chases in movies and on the news. Such chases are naturally exciting. But so many innocent drivers and pedestrians are killed as a result that some cities have banned car chases entirely.

But high-speed chases aren't the leading cause of death for routine offenders. Many traffic stops for a broken taillight or expired brake tag end up with a police officer shooting an unarmed person, often someone black or brown. And these are drivers who *didn't* flee, who *didn't* pose a threat.

But trained police officers are still human beings whose behavior can be influenced by fear and adrenalin. They are people who have grown up in a culture ensuring that even the most open-minded and humane among us have at least some lingering bias. When a life-or-death decision must be made in a split second, Sunday School lessons on "love thy neighbor" are replaced by the biological imperative to survive.

One of the most surprising truths I discovered as a Mormon missionary was that missionaries aren't particularly good people.

Hey, I'm happy to offer myself up as Exhibit A.

Unquestionably, some missionaries are great. But that's by no means a given.

One of my zone leaders in Rome took an immediate disliking to me—perhaps fully justified—and set out to aggravate me on a daily basis. He lit my trash can on fire. He took my one blanket in the middle of winter, leaving me shivering through the night. He deliberately dirtied every dish and utensil in the apartment, even ones we weren't using, on the days I was assigned to wash dishes.

Another elder in Sardinia was so abusive I was pushed to the verge of suicide. When I transferred to a new district, and one of the elders there learned who my previous companion had been, he held up a hand and said, "Wait. Let me guess. You hated his guts."

Years later, I contacted this former mission companion to resolve my lingering unhappiness over our time together. He was the only person I'd ever truly hated. I'd actually come close to pushing him off our balcony and had to leave the room to save us both.

I called him up in Idaho several years after returning to the States because I didn't want to carry that anger around for the rest of my life.

To his credit, the guy apologized. "I was going through a tough time," he explained. "I was gay and struggling a lot with it."

I was dumbfounded. "Well, *I* was struggling with being gay, too," I wanted to say, "and *I* wasn't an ass."

Angelic, clean-cut Mormon missionaries aren't always nice… or trustworthy… or even halfway decent human beings. Many of them have a variety of personal demons and end up abusing the people around them regularly, especially those over whom they assume any authority.

Do we truly expect that police officers and judges and the guy down the street carrying a concealed weapon have none of the same issues?

Or more?

Are the officers pulling over drivers for routine offenses justified in feeling a level of fear that leads them to kill "in self-defense"? Are they overreacting out of bias? Are they subconsciously—or even consciously—using the incident as an opportunity to hurt someone they consider "less than"?

Are they just angry?

"My companion was leaning over the balcony looking at something and fell."

With a simple policy change, we can avoid these emotionally charged debates altogether. More importantly, we can avoid the deadly consequences of both justified and unjustified fear, of animus that can be lethal yet never proven. If police officers are legitimately putting themselves at risk by stopping a driver for something minor, that traffic stop doesn't need to happen. Let the errant driver go, for God's sake.

Revenue from issuing tickets needn't drop. Unless there's an immediate need to stop a kidnapper or killer, officers can record the license plate (like cameras do at stoplights all the time) and mail a ticket to the offender. There's no point in a physical confrontation of any kind, even a mild, orderly one. Police departments not being forced to spend millions on investigations and settlements, and not suffering constant PR nightmares, must surely be worth something as well.

If we can't justify endangering lives in a car chase over minor violations, then we shouldn't keep endangering them during traffic stops for non-threatening offenses. Such stops are not worth the death of the police officer, the driver, or any passengers in the vehicle. While legitimate issues, carpool lane violations and failure to signal aren't felonies. These lapses certainly don't warrant execution without a trial. If "Police Lives Matter," why insist on endangering officers for such trivial infractions?

White people who shrug off these unnecessary escalations should remember that the police don't only use excessive force against people of color. When an officer in Arkansas signaled a pregnant white woman driving across a long bridge to pull over, she slowed down and turned on her emergency flashers, a legal way to show she was looking for a safe place to comply. But the officer was still so irritated she didn't stop immediately on a bridge with an almost non-existent shoulder that he deliberately rammed her car and flipped it over.

Her crime? She'd been going a few miles over the speed limit. Technically an infraction, not a crime, and one she'd stopped the moment she signaled she was cooperating with the officer and looking for a place to park.

If "All Lives Matter," why feel compelled to continue a policy which can only lead to additional injuries and deaths of both officers and civilians over petty offenses?

As a child attending my first big tent circus, I remember the announcer revealing that the trapeze artists were about to walk across the tightrope without a net. Even at that young age, I thought, "Do they really need to risk killing themselves just for a show?"

There are times police officers and other first responders do need to put their lives on the line. There are times when everyday civilians need to do it, too.

But there's no need for anyone to risk their life simply to reprimand someone over a broken taillight. Some officers have even pulled cars over simply because they were driving three miles *under* the speed limit along a corridor frequently used by drug traffickers. If the driver was being so careful not to attract attention, the officers reasoned, he was probably up to no good.

When officers can justify pulling over a car in perfect condition being driven without breaking even the most minor regulation, we have a problem with the status quo.

There are few perfect cops, or perfect missionaries, or perfect teachers, or perfect people of any kind. That's why the policies themselves are so important.

We must create a workable—and survivable—system despite everyday human failings.

Because of everyday human failings.

For the sake of those killed during routine traffic stops, we must cease all stops that don't involve reckless or intoxicated driving. "We've always done it this way" is no longer a valid rationale for sustaining a policy that inflicts so much unnecessary harm.

Let's ban all routine traffic stops.

First Responders: Police, Firefighters, and… Mental Health Officers?

Who do we think of when we hear the term "first responder"? Do we envision a doctor? A firefighter? A police officer?

Do we envision a SWAT team? A paramedic? An air marshal?

Or do we envision a civilian? After all, the first people who respond to almost every crime, natural disaster, or other traumatic event are almost always civilians.

At many workplaces, a few employees in each department or on each floor are given annual First Aid and CPR training, perhaps even defibrillator training. Some are given training in how to lead fire, earthquake, or tornado drills.

But something almost no firefighter is trained to do, almost no police officer, no paramedic, no SWAT team, no bank employee, is how to deal with a mental health crisis. It wouldn't hurt for most workplaces to require some basic training on the subject, but it can never match the training mental health professionals receive.

I saw online recently the image of a flier taped to a light pole. The designer had posed the following scenario and asked people to choose the correct answer: "You think someone is experiencing a mental health crisis and needs help. You call 9-1-1. Who shows up?"

There are four possible responses to this multiple-choice question.

a) An armed police officer
b) An armed police officer
c) An armed police officer
d) An armed police officer

Then rethinkportland.com concludes, "The answer is the problem. It's time to rethink community safety."

I'm confused by the pushback against this idea. Wouldn't most police officers *prefer* someone else take care of the mental illness calls? I know when I'm on the bus and a passenger boards, ranting and raving, I start praying to the universe. "Please don't let him see me. Please make him walk past. Please help—"

And then then fellow sits right beside me.

Sure, I manage to get through the following ten minutes before I reach my stop, or I pull the cord and climb off early, walking the rest of the way or waiting for the next bus. I'm sympathetic to the difficulties faced by folks with various mental health issues. I try to say something kind, engage or not engage as best I can guess will be more effective. But even though I understand that most of the unpleasant behaviors and outbursts aren't really their "fault," I still don't *want* to deal with the situation. The behaviors are still unsettling, still annoying, even if I don't blame the people doing them.

If I was a police officer trained to fight crime, and *not* trained to understand or address mental health crises, wouldn't I *want* another agency to take those calls?

If the problem is a mental health crisis, we should want the mental health crisis to be resolved, shouldn't we? We *shouldn't* want to kill the person in crisis. We *shouldn't* want the officer killing the person in crisis to be hounded and arrested and convicted. We *shouldn't* want riots over the killing of an unarmed person. We *shouldn't* want millions of our fellow Americans to feel unwanted in their own country.

To many Mormons and other evangelical Christians, addiction seems like a self-inflicted mental health issue and therefore somehow not deserving of treatment. Yet we have no problem believing obesity-caused heart problems are deserving. Or obesity-caused diabetes. We'd call an ambulance if an obese person was having a medical crisis.

Even as we managed to judge the person as a sinful glutton.

"Why do they keep doing this to themselves? They have no self-control. It's so, so sad."

An LDS friend of mine late in my Single Adult days was an addict. She never took part in a 12-step program, however, because what she was addicted to was drama.

"Did you *hear*?" she used to say the moment I picked up the phone.

"No. What?"

"Susan had an *affair* with a man at work!"

"OK."

"And she doesn't want to tell the bishop!"

"OK."

"What do you think about *that*?"

"Not much, to be honest."

"Me, either! Isn't she just *terrible*?"

What I'd meant was that I couldn't care less what Susan did or did not do with coworkers in private. Of course, by that point, I was already dating men, so sexual "impropriety" was pretty far down on my list of concerns.

Then this friend called me early one Tuesday morning. "Did you *hear*?" she asked.

"What?"

"We all felt so uncomfortable when you brought your boyfriend to Single Adult Family Home Evening last night."

"Uh huh."

"And after you left, we all felt worse and worse."

"OK."

"So we finally had to call the bishop to come cast out the evil spirit you brought!"

When we deliberately refuse to alleviate suffering, when we instead intentionally compound the suffering of others and as a result increase our own suffering, from an outside perspective, our behavior is incomprehensible.

Why would we go out of our way to create conditions where more and more people are forced into homelessness and in turn create trash dumps and cesspools throughout our communities?

Why do we make it difficult for people to get an education and rise out of poverty when uneducated, poor, and unemployed citizens by the millions only make everyone's life more challenging?

Why do we refuse to address bias and racism when it's abundantly clear that not doing so brings death, protests, riots, and plain old everyday misery across our nation?

None of it makes sense unless we reframe the question.

Are we so addicted to drama that we simply can't help ourselves? Will we keep snorting the meth of fear until our teeth rot? Will we keep injecting ourselves with the heroin of hatred until we're found dead with a needle in our arm?

"Defunding" the police in part simply means redirecting the funds necessary to address mental health crises to the folks trained to handle mental health crises. It's not taking anything away from "law and order." We adequately fund mental health programs so that many of these crises don't develop in the first place.

I regularly pay folks to tend my lawn because I don't want to do it myself. I accept that I must give these workers money to do what to me are unpleasant tasks. My neighbors benefit as well by no longer being burdened with the unsightly weeds in my yard. There are extremely few "front yard missionaries" going house to house tending people's yards for free. The task needs to be done. I either do it poorly, hating every minute of it, or I pay someone to do it for me. That's life.

Some people suggest we come up with a less threatening term than "defund the police," and if we can, that would be great. I learned in freshman composition class that even the best arguments often fail if authors can't reach their audience. But whatever term we use, "defund the police" or "reallocate certain public funds to more appropriate departments" (and doesn't *that* roll off the tongue smoothly!), we need to point out that we're freeing police officers to do what they're trained for. We're eliminating unpleasant tasks from their duties that most don't want to do anyway, that often end badly, that destroy their reputation and inflict unmeasurable harm across the community.

The end result of reassigning these mental health calls, of funding other programs and departments to address a multitude of social and mental health needs in every community, is that both the police and the public are better served. Folks who join the police force do so because serving the public is their goal. Paying mental health experts and social workers or other "agents" to reduce mental health crises or deal with them when they do occur is a win/win/win.

The people who don't allow themselves to understand this are just acting… crazy.

Too bad we don't have anyone trained we can send out to talk them down.

Let's Rehearse Anti-Racist Strategies

When my husband and I flew from Seattle to New Orleans to spend a few days with my father in rural Mississippi, we were mostly worried about how my homophobic father would react to our marriage. We weren't expecting to be treated to lunch at a restaurant shaped like Aunt Jemima. "Oh, my God," I whispered to my husband. "I hope there are no security cameras. I don't want any video of us going in here."

What I *could* have done was ask my father if we could eat somewhere else. But I didn't. Our relationship was already full of judgment, and I didn't want to add any of my own.

Time and again, I've found myself thrust unexpectedly into morally awkward positions, and 80% of the time, my behavior during these interactions has been shameful. I let things slide. So I decided to start practicing how to react in a wide variety of situations, realizing that most scenarios almost always involved complicated relationships. If it was easy to do the right thing, we'd all do it every time.

Thankfully, many people *do* in fact respond appropriately in most circumstances, but some of us need to commit ourselves more fully. And remaining committed requires preparation.

What do we say if the offensive remark or action comes from our boss? Would we react differently if it came from our spouse? Our children? How do we react when the person is someone further removed but who we still have to interact with regularly, like a neighbor or coworker? What do we say if it's a good friend? A casual acquaintance? Our professor? Our child's teacher? An extended family member?

Even if the person we must address is a complete stranger on the bus or in a store, the situation is still complicated. Will the stranger flip out and physically attack us?

There will *always* be a risk in confronting racism or sexism or homophobia or body shaming or xenophobia or anti-Semitism or any other type of oppression. If we haven't prepared for the moment, we will too often let the opportunity to address it slip away.

At one workplace, two black teenage boys came into our store and began behaving in a way that irritated my boss. He angrily asked them to leave. They refused and began behaving in a more antagonizing fashion. They weren't trying to steal anything, weren't posing any danger. They didn't even say anything threatening. Everyone was simply angry.

My boss ordered me to call the police. I hesitated, knowing that these kids could end up dead over nothing. But the argument continued, and when my boss looked back and saw I still hadn't picked up the phone, he ordered me again to call.

Could I have refused? Could I have motioned my boss over to talk to him privately? Could I have pretended to call the police but not really punched in any numbers? Could I have said loudly enough for the teens to hear that I'd hit the emergency button, without actually pressing it? In the moment, there is no time to consider the range of possibilities, to debate the pros and cons of each. I picked up the phone and called 9-1-1. When the dispatcher asked what the emergency was, I said, "My boss wants the police to come because there are some teenagers causing trouble."

As soon as I said the words, I realized how utterly pathetic my agreement to place the call had been. "Just following orders" didn't work as justification during the Nuremberg trials, and whatever the legal consequences to me now for complying, clearly what I'd done was wrong.

But what if I got fired for not obeying? I was barely paying my monthly bills as it was.

My risk: being reprimanded or losing my job.

Risk to those teens: being arrested, beaten, tasered, shot.

I had the privilege, though, as a white male, of being more likely than some to find another job, even in my mid-fifties. I could mitigate my risk. I'd seen enough cell phone video to know that young black men could be killed even if cooperating peacefully and, given the escalation I'd already seen taking place in the store, peaceful cooperation wasn't likely. It became clear that if I wasn't willing to give up a tiny bit of my privilege and take the risks associated with standing up against oppression, I couldn't consider myself an ally.

Or even a decent human being.

Thankfully, the teens left, and the police never came. But what *might* have happened because I made the wrong choice?

I saw a Jewish cartoon once showing two Jews lined up against a wall about to be shot. One man calls out to the leader of the firing squad, "Can I have a cigarette?"

The other condemned man whispers nervously to him, "Don't make trouble."

The situation in this country is already dire. The option not to make trouble doesn't exist. Trouble is here.

The realization that I needed to change didn't carry with it the knowledge of how to accomplish such change. I simply knew I wasn't good at figuring out what to do or say with only a second's notice. I was going to need preparation and practice.

The first order of business was to brainstorm a list of possible scenarios. Then do some research to discover other situations. I keep a folder of every job interview question I've ever been asked or seen in articles, along with anecdotes and other notes to use in response. I try to envision anything a job interviewer might throw my way. There's always something unexpected, but because I've practiced so many different scenarios, I can usually come up with *something* without floundering too badly.

When I worked at a credit union, I was required to take a "fun" class where the participants took turns playing difficult customers and the rest of us had to find not only tactful but commercially successful ways of dealing with them.

As a Mormon missionary in Italy, my companions and I practiced how to convert any “No” at the door into an invitation to teach a lesson.

In some ways, reaching the hearts of people who may not even be aware of their bias requires some degree of sales. We’re “selling” more accurate information, better behaviors and policies.

We can decide on appropriate responses to acts of oppression by studying alone in our room, or working with a friend, our spouse, our entire family. We can come up with “friendly” ways to nudge a conversation. We can be firm and direct. We can explain why a certain word or action is inappropriate. The responses will be different depending on who is involved and the severity of the problem. We can review our notes regularly so we don’t fall out of practice.

If we’re responding every time it’s necessary, though, we aren’t very likely to have an opportunity to fall out of practice.

Some folks get together for book club meetings or movie nights. We might form a group of friends or neighbors into an anti-racist club.

Role-playing may be embarrassing at first. If it is, that’s only proof that the real thing will be even more uncomfortable, something we won’t be able to handle without rehearsing.

We can also prepare a Plan B, how to approach someone an hour or a day after the incident. Even that's better than not addressing it at all.

As with any skill, we'll become more proficient over time. Blundering is better than silence if we sincerely want to shape a more equitable society.

The other day, a friend in another country told me he understood why Trump wanted a wall along our border with Mexico. "Legal immigration is one thing," he said, "but you can't just let anyone walk in who wants to."

We've been friends for years, I really like the guy, and I'm aware our relationship has been threatened in the past when I stood up for the right of the terminally ill to have access to physician-assisted death, over my friend's occasional sexist jokes, and over several other issues. So even if he wasn't my boss or my spouse or a neighbor I'd see every day, even if we already had a history of broaching difficult subjects, I immediately felt that familiar "awkward," "complicated" worry about what to say.

But I was prepared. "You know," I said, "thousands of those in detention camps were *legally* requesting asylum. Hundreds and hundreds of children were separated from their parents. The detention centers deliberately didn't keep track of those children, and many are lost forever from the system and can never be reunited with their parents. *That's* Trump's border policy."

And I had plenty to say if we wanted to talk about Obama's border policy, or U.S. immigration policy in general over the past few decades.

My friend didn't respond, and really, his response is to some extent irrelevant. Obviously, we want to persuade other people to understand more and as a result behave better, but the behavior we *must* change—the only behavior we can control—is our own.

Most of us aren't *always* silent. Many times, we stand up at the right moment and say or do the right thing. But too often it's hit or miss, and that's just not good enough anymore.

Being well-meaning, having good intentions, and "believing" in equality aren't sufficient. We must confront oppression in the moment. If not every time, then certainly a lot more than we're doing now. So let's make that improved behavior possible and start practicing.

Resisting Bigotry One Day at a Time

I've never drunk an alcoholic beverage. I've never used illicit drugs. And yet I understand something about facing chronic, destructive conditions like alcoholism, and not only because I've known many people in recovery programs. Just as an alcoholic sober for thirty years can never say she's "cured," I must confront my chronic, implicit biases one day at a time. It may get easier along the way, but there will never be a point at which I can declare I no longer harbor any bias. That doesn't need to feel like defeat, it doesn't have to seem pointless or hopeless. It's simply an acknowledgement of reality. Folks I know in AA and NA accept reality every day without losing joy in life. In fact, most enjoy life even more after acknowledging this fundamental truth.

Jim was the first man I dated who attended AA meetings twice a week. He sponsored a newly sober man who lived with him. While I didn't date Jim more than a couple of months, it was long enough to understand that alcoholics faced trials I couldn't imagine. It struck me as horrific to live every day knowing you could make a mistake that might have life-altering consequences. Jim's roommate began drinking again after only a few months of sobriety, was kicked out of the house, and that was the last I heard of him. I decided it was too risky to date anyone in AA again. Jim died several years later of emphysema.

Staying sober didn't help him kick his addiction to nicotine.

Similarly, I have friends and family who have made incredible strides in addressing their bias toward LGBTQ folks or toward women, who still cannot face their chronic prejudice against Native Americans or African Americans or Muslims. In the show *Mom*, Christy is reluctant to face the undeniable fact that even after six years of sobriety, she is still addicted to gambling. She doesn't *want* to have to deal with anything else. "I can't be this broken," she says. But she finally starts facing that separate addiction one day at a time as well.

Frank told me on our first date that he "used" to drink but was sober now. Wary, I kept some emotional distance, but we'd only been dating a month or so when I received some unsettling news from the HIV center about my most recent test. I was trying to join a vaccine trial but had been disqualified.

I called Frank, the only person I was ready to confide in. I knew he was positive and could help me sort through my feelings. I agreed to pick him up that evening so we could talk.

He was drunk when he came to the door.

Just as I discovered I could never really trust him again after that, many black folks or members of other oppressed groups often have difficulty fully trusting white people. My boyfriend didn't drink "on purpose" or to deliberately hurt me, but that didn't change how his behavior affected me at a time when I was vulnerable.

Frank gave up drinking again a few days later, but six weeks after that, he went on another week-long drinking binge. He was "sober" again for six more weeks, went on another binge, and committed to abstinence yet again.

He died a year later, holed up in his apartment on a drinking binge. Cirrhosis.

Not everyone can maintain sobriety. Or their commitment to justice and equality. One can't just coast along. It takes work, probably more than the traditional 12 Steps. And many people who falter lose their jobs or their standing in the community as a result. J.K. Rowling's insistence on denying the reality of trans men and women may not ruin her career, but she's certainly losing a great many fans. A Manhattan woman lost her job after faking a hysterical phone call to the police upon seeing a black birdwatcher in Central Park. The CEO of a successful business was caught ranting at an Asian family in a California restaurant. People behaving poorly and publicly don't always face backlash, but sometimes, they lose a great deal. Yet people continue to do and say horrific things, even knowing they're on camera, because they can't admit they have a problem.

When dating another alcoholic, a man who'd been sober over twenty-five years, I attended an Al-Anon meeting to learn a bit more about how a sober person could manage relationships with non-sober folks. Many of us have family members who refuse to acknowledge either their chemical addictions or their subconscious prejudices, and that refusal makes it difficult for us to maintain functioning relationships with them. There may be no formal Bias Anonymous meetings, but we can find other ways to support one another as we deal regularly with the destructive, hurtful people in our lives. Almost everyone has a bigotaholic in our family who makes it hard to be thankful at Thanksgiving.

A friend of mine, sober for twenty years and married for eighteen, grew frustrated that his husband could have a relaxing drink any evening he wanted but he couldn't. He finally decided he simply didn't believe it was healthy to never allow himself even one drink.

Most of us know of someone who falls after many years of success. We're baffled. "Why did he throw it all away?"

It's mostly because people forget that we are *never cured* of addiction. Remaining clean and sober requires constant vigilance.

A white friend of mine in his seventies (and let me be honest—I've never had any deep friendships with folks who weren't white) told me he'd been trying his entire life not to be racist, but these protests and riots for Black Lives Matter made him just give up. He doesn't like black people, and he's not going to try to fight that feeling anymore.

What must it be like to attend weekly AA meetings for thirty years, thirty-five, and still know you could relapse? What must it be like to have made amends for the many terrible things you did while drunk or high and know that you could still louse up every relationship you value, that you could still end up drunk and homeless after retirement?

My grandmother almost lost her faith in God at the end of her life because God had seen fit to give her non-smoking sister lung cancer.

What must it be like to lose faith in ourselves, in the possibility of peace and a better future for humanity?

Knowing that whatever "success" I achieve in resisting my biases can never guarantee a permanent cure is frightening, disappointing, even a bit depressing. But what, really, are my options? I can continue to confront my biases one day at a time or I can give up.

Given the nature of this chronic condition, I can't truly predict where I'll be five years from now, or three, or two. What I do know is that "just for today," I'm going to remember I have a problem, one I didn't choose but one I must deal with anyway, and I'm going to resist giving in, facing the challenge one day at a time.

White Racist for Black Lives Matter

When I relocated to Seattle after Hurricane Katrina, I encountered what at first seemed a less racist culture than I'd experienced in New Orleans. Then I noticed that my coworkers limited their racist comments until our black manager left the room. One even said he wished the military would dump airplane fuel on black protesters.

But *I* wasn't like that. I watched movies like *The Hate U Give* and *Get Out.* I donated to the United Negro College Fund. I read James Baldwin. *I* wasn't racist.

At another job, employees were asked to take an assessment test that determined levels of unconscious bias. My results showed I had a "strong preference" for white people over black. And I took the assessment *right after* participating in two Black Lives Matter protests.

It felt like taking a DNA test and discovering I was adopted. I'm not who I thought I was.

But my bias doesn't prevent me from recognizing the urgent need to dismantle institutional racism and to support the efforts of those more knowledgeable than I am to do so.

For years, I've known about the "black national anthem." When I heard it a few Saturdays ago during a rally at Othello Playground, I didn't even recognize the melody. I'm 60 years old and never bothered to look it up.

I've learned over the past several weeks that it's not possible to be non-racist in a society that shapes us to be racist every day of our lives. I'm now finally trying to be anti-racist.

At the rally, I held up my handmade sign, the words, "Black Trans Lives Matter" on one side and "LGBTQ for BLM" on the other. It was Pride month, after all.

Other signs insisted we "End Qualified Immunity" and "Say her name!" A white man's hat bore the words "Veterans for Peace" while a white woman held a sign asking us to "Amplify Black Voices."

Probably 400 people were at the rally, far fewer than the thousands at other local protests over the past few weeks. I saw a white friend at the park, an older woman with bursitis. A longtime activist, she told me, "I can't run anymore, and when you know the police might attack you for no reason, you want to be able to run." Another white friend was there, too, walking unsteadily with a cane.

A white counter-protester started shouting from the street using a megaphone. The speaker on the stand carried on while about thirty folks in the crowd blocked the man from approaching, drowning out his intrusion with chants of "Black Lives Matter!"

I tensed when I heard sirens in the distance, growing louder until… they passed by on nearby MLK. Several protesters sighed in relief. I expect most of the white folks at the rally were used to *seeing* police violence, not worrying about becoming the recipients of it. These past few weeks, some of us were likely feeling this particular fear for the first time.

I remembered a photo I'd seen online, a black man with a sign explaining, "We aren't trying to start a race war. We're trying to end one."

A young woman on the stand read some poetry. Other young women performed a dance. Several speakers gave short talks, the emphasis at today's rally the lives of black women. A Somali talked of the retaliation she'd faced at work for speaking out about unsafe conditions during the pandemic.

Then all the non-black folks—about 300 of us—were ordered to the street, the black protesters asked to remain near the stand. On Othello, a group of bicycle riders raced up and down the block, guiding the white, Asian, Indian, and Latinx protesters to line up along both curbs. We were to lock arms and act as a shield against any counter-protesters who might try to break through and interfere with the black marchers. "Alternate which direction you're facing," one of the riders instructed us, "so you can be on the alert to danger approaching from any direction."

Another bicycle rider zipped by. "Remember why you're here," he said.

A white woman on the other side of the street stepped onto her porch with a lighted candle and held it out toward us for moral support.

After fifteen or twenty minutes, the black protesters walked over from the main part of the rally. They headed west toward MLK, and the non-black allies kept on both sides and behind as they marched toward the police station a few blocks away to make their demands known… again.

When I returned home, I checked my social media and saw several new racist posts from my family. It was disappointing, but I also felt hope.

Because while I'm white, and still strongly biased, I'm one of many who know that Black Lives Matter.

Go and Sin a Little Less

As a Mormon missionary in Rome, I proudly told "investigators" that we had a living prophet with direct access to God. Latter-day Saints were privy to modern revelation and therefore not fumbling about blindly like everyone else, struggling to analyze texts from the ancient past to figure out how to live.

Yet it seems LDS leaders continually refuse to move into the present, much less the future. "We won't be buffeted by the changing whims of society!" Instead, we not only condone but also canonize sin.

Living prophet or no living prophet, that's not good.

Sure, apologists say, Brigham Young supported African slavery and wanted to enslave Native Americans as well, but we must remember he was a man of his times.

True enough, but even in the mid-1800s, quite a few less prophetic people understood that slavery was immoral. There ended up being a whole war about it.

If we want to give early LDS Church leaders a pass by putting their racist behaviors and policies into "context," that still doesn't absolve our current leaders. Just as it was impossible for Adam and Eve to commit a sin by eating of the Tree of Knowledge of Good and Evil because by definition they *couldn't* know the difference between right and wrong at the time they partook, we still point out that they committed a "transgression."

They broke a commandment, whether or not they were "guilty," and according to LDS theology there were serious consequences that continue to this day.

Likewise, even if some of our earlier leaders made poor decisions, which all humans do sometimes, we need to accept that these "transgressions" can't simply be ignored. There have been and continue to be horrific consequences.

As Carol Lynn Pearson so beautifully wrote in her song "My Story" for the musical *My Turn on Earth*, repentance allows us to erase a bad line from our story, sometimes a bad page, even a bad chapter. "Or more."

Hiding our history adds to the problem, however, rather than lessens it, because it's a refusal to address the ongoing damage created by not making amends.

We shouldn't erase our past. But we can and should change the present.

We know the LDS Church can do so because it's done so before.

We disavowed Joseph Smith's polygamy and polyandry.

We disavowed polygamy for the rest of the Church with the 1890 Manifesto.

We disavowed polygamy again in 1904 with the Second Manifesto.

We disavowed polygamy once more in 1933 with the Third Manifesto.

We disavowed beards when David O. McKay became Prophet.

We disavowed the priesthood and temple ban against Black members.

We eliminated the Indian Placement Program.

We moved away from one-piece garments.

We eliminated death oaths from the temple ceremony.

We eliminated Home Teaching and Visiting Teaching.

We disavowed the "Mormon" label.

We gave up the Boy Scouts.

We've even now decided to get rid of temple murals.

Yet somehow, it's beyond the pale to change the name of Brigham Young University. We couldn't possibly rename it Restoration U or Latter-day Saint U or United Order U.

Oh, that's right, we got rid of the United Order, too.

When we're asked to replace problematic names of institutions or relocate controversial statues to museums, and our response is, "Get over it," we're not only declaring that racism isn't a sin now, but we're also saying it was never even a transgression at any time.

The whole point of having modern revelation is to be able to adapt to changing circumstances and not be stuck in the past.

Other religions change and adapt over the years, and it hasn't hurt them. Catholics gave up the Inquisition, gave up indulgences, gave up their insistence to only conduct mass in Latin. Jews no longer practice animal sacrifice. Anglicans now have female priests.

When Mormons see these changes, they often scoff. "*We* don't have to change. *We* have the truth." Of course, every religion believes it's right, but even the "true" Mormon Church has reduced the length of missionary service from three years to two, has lowered the age for missionaries, has changed the role of women in the temple, has modified the rules for excommunication.

Mormons have even altered some of the wording in the Book of Mormon.

Without a doubt, we can address bias and racism more fully.

Jesus said, "Go and sin no more." As encouraging as that sounds, it's unlikely any of us, even the top leaders of the LDS Church, will achieve perfection in this life. But we can all at least "Go and sin a little less."

Because while anything inappropriate we might have said or done in the past *may* have been no more than a transgression at the time, now that we know better—*and we do*—not to move away from those errors constitutes full-fledged sin.

So let's choose to make just a little more progress toward a perfection that can only be reached if we actively move toward it.

Section 3: Expanding Social Justice to All

Don't Feed the Humans: Criminalizing Compassion

In recent months, government agents have begun implementing a new tactic to deny illegal immigrants and desperate refugees the opportunity to find a safe haven in the U.S. In addition to arresting and detaining immigrants, even those entering legally and making legal requests for asylum, government agencies have begun arresting anyone daring to provide food or water to those crossing one of the most dangerous deserts in our hemisphere. We're not talking about forcing volunteer aid workers to pay a nuisance fine. These humanitarians are being charged with felonies and face up to twenty years in prison.

Agents claim that providing water to a pregnant woman is an act of human smuggling. Of course, no one is fooled by this attempt at spinning the narrative. While actual human smuggling can rightly be condemned, offering compassion shouldn't be criminalized. When charges of smuggling appear too ridiculous to sustain, agents switch to another charge. They arrest humanitarians providing water with littering and abandonment of property.

A zero-tolerance policy against littering in the Sonoran desert might be more believable if deliberate government shutdowns didn't allow mountains of garbage to accumulate in our parks, if oil and toxic chemicals weren't contaminating many of our rivers, lakes, and coastal waters, if city streets weren't overflowing with trash all across the country. In the impoverished White Center neighborhood where I work, just inches outside Seattle city limits, public trash cans have been set up in multiple locations, but there is no regular pick up. During the three years I've worked in the area, I've seen garbage overflowing from every can, week after week after week. Birds pick through it. Homeless people pick through it. Undocumented immigrants, I suspect, pick through it as well.

It's almost as if the purpose of the trash cans isn't to keep the area clean but to offer proof that the destitute cause their own problems. "These people are animals. Look at the filth they live in." Poor and homeless people obviously don't have the capacity to cart off garbage from public receptacles to the appropriate government facilities. But this denial of sanitary conditions to the poor isn't accidental. It's not an oversight. It's an effective way to dehumanize. Poor people just aren't worth the nominal funds it would take to empty their trash cans, and they hear that message loud and clear.

But by golly, if someone hands a dehydrated child a plastic jug of water that might be left behind in the desert, we must do whatever is necessary to stamp out such reckless behavior!

That child may not understand English, but she hears the message America is sending her just as clearly—our zero-tolerance policies give her a zero-value life.

Even if there were some way to justify the criminalization of humanitarian aid to non-citizens, there seems to be even less justification for arresting people in dozens of cities across the U.S. who offer food to our steadily increasing homeless population. Government officials claim these laws are designed to prevent the spread of disease, but one wonders why, if the health of homeless men, women, and children is their primary concern, these same officials don't ensure that health by distributing food through "appropriate" means, furnishing adequate shelter, or, at the very least, offering guaranteed healthcare. Providing medical services, after all, seems like a better way to safeguard health than denying them food.

No one is deceived by the pretense that criminalizing aid to the poor, destitute, and dying is to "protect" the vulnerable. The goal is clearly to penalize empathy, drive compassion into the closet, make good, decent people afraid to act humanely toward their fellow man. If people are forced to worry enough about themselves, are made to fear banding together to help one another, they are easier to control.

"Intellectuals" are among the first to be imprisoned when totalitarian governments rise to power. Humanitarians seem to be near the top of the list as well, at least for our totalitarian-wannabe leaders. When "Don't Feed the Humans" becomes the moral equivalent of "Don't Feed the Pigeons," we know we are in serious trouble.

To protect our nation's standing in the world, to protect the character of our citizens, and to protect human life itself, we must stop criminalizing compassion.

Cages, Camps, Jails, and Prisons

I was first convicted in a court of law at the age of sixteen.

The District Attorney had walked up to me during breakfast in a school cafeteria, staged a crime, and had me arrested. He was desperate, he apologized to me later, to try a case.

The first part of the trial went in my favor. I was able to respond to my questioning on the stand with pointed quips that showed I was being framed.

But then we recessed for lunch. And somehow, after we reconvened, the atmosphere in the courtroom changed. Every question seemed more restrictive. I was given parameters for my responses that would no longer permit me to explain the situation as it had actually developed. I'd always been a goody-two-shoes, I thought. How could this be happening to me? I realized with a feeling of dread that I wasn't going to escape.

"I'm innocent!" I concluded.

The verdict was "Guilty," and I was quickly sentenced.

After the trial, a judge who'd been in the courtroom but who hadn't presided over the proceedings came up to me. "I'm so sorry. I saw what happened in the cafeteria, but because I couldn't be impartial, I had to recuse myself."

"If you saw," I countered, "shouldn't you have been on the stand as a witness in my defense?"

Thank God this was only Boys State. An untucked shirt wasn't going to go on my permanent record. Even if we didn't understand our instructions perfectly during the week-long program to teach high school students more about politics, I had my first inkling that not every convicted felon was truly guilty of the crimes for which they were serving time.

My next conviction came when I was 27. The high priests in my Mormon stake held a Church tribunal. The disciplinary council was, naturally, called a Court of Love. I recognized Orwellian terms after reading *1984* for the first time a few years earlier. I was accused by the stake presidency of having sex with other men. This time I *was* in fact "guilty" and was subsequently excommunicated. "Please take off your garments," the stake president told me.

I had known this would be the verdict and the first part of my "sentence," so I was not wearing my Mormon underwear that evening and had none to remove. Unlike my sentence at Boys State, this time my "punishment" was freedom, but I still learned something important.

Not all laws determining criminality were just.

And sentencing was sometimes more about humiliation than reform.

The United States has the largest prison population per capita in the world. We send far too many innocent men and women to prison daily. Even guilty criminals often spend two or more years in jail waiting for their day in court.

So much for "a speedy trial."

Public defenders have caseloads of 100 clients, 150, 180, or more.

We threaten vulnerable people with such horrific sentences that even innocent people plead guilty to get a "reduced" sentence of a mere seven or eight years.

And yet, if we've made society safer by this "tough on crime" approach, most people in this country don't seem to feel it. We buy more and more guns every day for "self-defense." We put people in cages, in camps, in detention centers. We put people in prison. We deport people with no criminal record because we fear they might one day commit a crime.

We label as criminals fathers trying to protect their children, mothers trying to escape rape.

We put people in jail for fifty years for possessing half an ounce of pot.

Do we really think we're making the world a better place by destroying millions of lives? Our prisons are hardly institutions where inmates learn healthy social skills, where they earn a useful education to pursue gainful careers upon release. Some do, of course, but the general prison environment ensures that won't be the norm. Even California inmates who risk their lives fighting forest fires for a dollar an hour are often excluded from employment as firefighters after their release.

Crowded prisons in Texas, Florida, Louisiana, Alabama, and many other states often have no air conditioning for inmates, even if there is AC for staff, even when there's AC for the pigs on the prison pig farm, and even when the heat index in the inmate living areas reaches 150 degrees.

If it "costs too much" to treat millions of inmates humanely, perhaps we shouldn't be imprisoning millions of inmates.

Americans have a deep, almost addictive need to punish, but we need to start being practical. We have decades and decades of evidence that our prison-industrial complex isn't making our communities healthier.

A friend once asked me, "Do you want to be right or do you want to be happy?" It was a question his sponsor in AA had asked him years earlier.

Sometimes, insisting on getting our way, demanding that others acknowledge our superiority during an argument, guarantees that we *won't* be happy. So what's our real goal?

Punishing more people than any other country in the world hasn't made us happy. If it had, we wouldn't need to "Make America Great Again." We'd already be there. Has putting record numbers of people in for-profit prisons over the last couple of years, separating parents from their children, giving those kids away to strangers, made us happier as a nation? Has it made us feel safer?

There are bad people out there who need to be taken off the streets. But if we already imprison a larger percentage of our population than any other country on Earth, and we still feel we have too many criminals running loose, something is fundamentally flawed about our culture. And that something clearly isn't being solved by mass incarceration.

Maybe helping people rather than trying as hard as we can to destroy them might produce better results. It seems to work in most places it's tried, in isolated U.S. municipalities and in many other nations around the world.

Do we want to be right or do we want to be happy?

Chimney Sweeps, Typesetters, Tobacco Farmers, and the Police

Many police officers, hearing the growing demand to "Defund the Police," are afraid for their future. Already feeling under siege every time they make a drug arrest or respond to a domestic violence call, they now also face the worry of soon being out of work.

We've all heard the saying, "A cornered animal is the most dangerous." In addition to internalized bias, some of the violence officers commit rises, one way or another, out of an instinctive fight or flight response. That's partly why so many officers brazenly commit unprovoked acts of violence on camera for millions to see, even in response to a movement accusing them of unprovoked violence.

Society has reached a tipping point where we have no choice but to reduce the number of officers in our communities, reduce their military equipment, and reduce the number of tasks for which they're responsible. All of us, whether we're "pro" or "anti" police, need to understand that over the past couple of centuries certain jobs were unavoidably lost to technological and societal advance, and some tasks assigned to the police are facing the same natural outcome.

Slave traders adapted quickly to trading other "cargo" after the abolition of slavery.

At certain points over the years, rat catchers, ice cutters, switchboard operators, human alarm clocks, and bowling alley pinsetters had a difficult time finding other work, but whatever the difficulty, they did so because their former jobs simply ceased to exist.

Before there were Creosote Sweeping Logs, young children were hired to climb up chimneys to clean them out so that accumulated soot wouldn't catch fire and destroy the building. It was a dangerous job that often left children maimed or dead. Newspaper and book publishers for hundreds of years hired typesetters who could lay out moveable type—backwards—so that readers could enjoy their publications.

Elevator operators are a thing of the past. Gas station attendants only work in isolated areas where laws were directly established to preserve their jobs despite the nationwide and global move forward.

We need to realize that many jobs in our police departments, judicial system, and prison system are also obsolete, regardless of our feelings about that fact. To make even a rocky transition possible, we must find alternative income for these workers.

When automation replaced tens of thousands of manufacturing jobs, the workers were left to rot, turning once beautiful cities in the Rust Belt into hellholes. If that's the prospect police officers or others affected by a Defund the Police movement face, we can be sure they'll fight to the death to protect their ability to provide for their families. Can we really blame them?

When I hear tobacco farmers complain that anti-smoking campaigns threaten their livelihood, I wonder why they just don't plant different crops. It's not as if we're taking away their farms. But there's an infrastructure in place to make it easier for them to continue producing a deadly product.

Coal miners fight to keep their industry alive, even though victory means working in unsafe, often miserable conditions. It's just that the alternative is unemployment and poverty. While corporate owners fight for oil and gas drilling out of a desire to accumulate vast fortunes, the workers they employ just want to feed their children. If we don't give those workers an alternative, how will they be able join the fight to mitigate the worst consequences of global warming?

A tenth of the workers hired to build the Panama Canal were killed during its construction. Even those who survived faced almost untold suffering. Many fully realized this going in.

But what other choice did they have?

Physicians used to diagnose diabetes by tasting the urine of their patients. It's why the official name of the condition is *diabetes mellitus*—*mellitus* means "honeyed" or "sweet" in Latin.

Humans have a natural tendency to be wary of change, but when the advantages of a particular technology or policy or philosophy become apparent, we cannot be kept away from it. I typed my first Master's thesis on a typewriter. When I learned my margins were a quarter of an inch off and that I couldn't graduate until my 120-page thesis was submitted properly, I quickly adapted to word processing.

Drivers adjusted from paper maps to GPS systems. People transitioned quickly from beepers to cell phones. Paper map makers and beeper manufacturers may have faced a reduction in their ranks, but other jobs developed to replace them. And that is the key ingredient to a successful push to reduce our bloated police force and mass incarceration system.

Would it be cost effective to close coal mines and instead provide a Universal Basic Income to displaced coal miners? What's the cost of unemployment, both in terms of unemployment payments and in the ravaging effects of poverty on a community? What's the cost of providing little or no alternative in job opportunities to police officers and prison employees?

Black and brown communities are those most impacted by the climate crisis, so without racial justice, we cannot create meaningful solutions to this global emergency.

We cannot adequately confront the pandemic or other health crises without guaranteeing universal healthcare.

We can't make measurable progress in reducing or defeating police brutality unless we also combat economic injustice at the same time. We must, at the very least, offer tuition-free college and vocational training to give displaced workers in every field an opportunity to move to professions that can benefit them personally. Only then will they be willing to make the changes that also benefit society as a whole.

I've worked in retail, in education, in banking, and in civil service. Those weren't all voluntary moves on my part. I did what I had to do when workplace opportunities shifted. Most of us face career changes at least once during our lifetime. If we want police and correctional officers to be on the right side of history in dismantling systemic and institutional racism, it will be easier if we're allies, even reluctant ones, rather than enemies.

A Universal Basic Income, tuition-free college and vocational training, and universal healthcare that includes mental healthcare, will reduce poverty and the crime so often associated with it, reducing the need for all those police officers and prisons to begin with. These policies will also help us mitigate the effects of climate change. And they'll lead us toward greater racial and economic justice. For a Defund the Police campaign to be successful, we must make it part of a larger package to bring about social justice.

Better Off Dead

Those on the left sometimes mock Christian conservatives for their political attacks against undocumented immigrants at the US/Mexico border. "Did Christ say, 'Hate thy neighbor as thyself?'"

But it's not all mockery. When it seems that conservatives *want* immigrants to die of thirst in the desert or be forced to return to their native countries where many will be murdered, bewildered humanitarians ask, "This is Christian behavior?"

Unfortunately, for some Christians, it is.

Watching *Lampedusa*, a mini-series illustrating the situation with illegal immigration into southern Italy, I had a flashback to my days as a Mormon. Not simply because I'd volunteered two years as an LDS missionary in that country but rather the result of my reaction to a certain "sweet" scene.

When a woman raped by a human smuggler gives birth to the child of her rapist, she wants nothing to do with the newborn. We've already seen one of the traffickers shoot and kill her husband, have watched as the pregnant widow was locked in a shed in Libya with other refugees, watched the woman almost drown while crossing the Mediterranean, watched as part of the refugee center in Lampedusa is burned by rioters.

So when a worker picks up the crying infant and places it on her mother's chest, and the mother finally embraces the baby, as viewers we're supposed to feel hope.

But *my* reaction was, "This woman is severely, permanently damaged. She will never recover emotionally. She'd be better off dead."

That's when I had the flashback. As a Mormon, I was taught that the only purpose of Earth life was to get a body that would later be resurrected. There's even a popular Mormon song, "Everybody Ought to Have a Body." The only other purpose for "coming to Earth" is to be tested. Some of my friends envied children who died before they turned eight (the Age of Accountability) because dying that young automatically qualified them for the highest degree of the Celestial Kingdom.

"He died at seven, lucky bastard."

When someone was killed in a terrible accident or died a few months after their spouse or child's untimely death, we said, 'At least they're not suffering anymore. They're better off on the Other Side.'"

Whenever a mourner cried at a funeral, we whispered behind their backs. "If they truly understood the Gospel, they'd be rejoicing."

Those lucky dead people had finished their tests. They'd gotten their bodies and were done with misery. Anything awkward or superficially sad about their demise would be "taken care of" during the Millennium.

Many conservative American Christians honestly don't consider the deaths of undocumented immigrants a terrible crisis. Some people, they feel, are better off dead.

Lampedusa offers American viewers a chance to see many of the same atrocities in our own immigration system in a way that allows us some emotional distance. The islanders complaining about the impact on tourism look petty. The bureaucracy tying the hands of rescuers feels oppressively corrupt. But, hey, what do we expect of southern Italy, the place where the Mafia was born?

Some of the rescuers in Lampedusa grow exhausted and want to give up, understanding that more people die every day than they can ever hope to save. It's easier to move to the mainland and forget the suffering of these strangers.

Nemer, an immigrant who leads a hunger strike in the detention center, is written into the screenplay too simplistically. He's a virtual saint. We're supposed to see how good and deserving he is. But that depiction distorts reality—people deserve to be helped not because they're wonderful but because they're human.

Likewise, we get crosscut scenes with Daki, a young boy separated from his mother and sister, who remain locked up in the Libyan shed with the pregnant widow. Daki keeps breaking out of the detention camp to steal so he can help his family pay for their passage. Meanwhile, we see his mother and sister back in northern Africa, terrified and abused by their traffickers.

During the course of the mini-series, we watch as boat after boat of immigrants sinks before reaching Italy. Sometimes, the Italian Coast Guard arrives in time. Other times, all they find are bodies floating in the sea.

We watch an anti-immigrant tour boat guide who accidentally comes upon drowning immigrants. He's horrified to see the suffering in front of him and jumps in to save a woman who has sunk beneath the surface. The guide's heart turns from hate to love through this one profound experience.

Simplistic.

Finally, Daki's mother and sister board the last boat from Libya. But before they can reach Lampedusa, a storm develops unexpectedly and the overcrowded boat starts taking on water. The traffickers begin pushing people overboard to lighten the load. Those who won't go without a fight are shot and dumped into the sea.

Daki's mother and sister end up in the Mediterranean, in near-total darkness, treading water as the storm rages. And the Coast Guard is too far away to help.

Earlier in the series, a detention worker says, "Deliberately making the lives of people more miserable won't deter them. They have no choice but to leave their homes."

At the same time, as American viewers, detached because all this is happening somewhere else, we also see how this island community is overrun by destitute immigrants. The impact is real.

What we understand is that the solution to suffering isn't amplification of suffering. Misery, it turns out, is bad domestic policy. It's also bad international policy. If we want people to stay in Syria or Mexico or Senegal or Guatemala, what we need to do is make life viable for them *there*.

We stop overthrowing democratically elected leaders. We stop supporting authoritarians because they're good for US trade.

Closing credits for the show reveal that Lampedusa took in over 153,000 immigrants in one year. More than 4000 drowned that year alone in the attempt to reach its shores. The producers weren't able to hire enough extras to depict the sinking of a single boat in 2013 that left 366 bodies floating in the sea.

Refugees are fleeing terror and war and poverty. And in the coming years, those numbers will only be augmented by climate change.

Making life miserable for the desperate won't solve the problem undocumented immigrants pose. Neither will ignoring it. Or choosing another show to watch.

Shrugging our shoulders with a "They're better off dead" won't help, either.

Despite its flaws, *Lampedusa* is worth viewing. As the captain of one of the Coast Guard ships says at the conclusion, "Whatever your reasons for blocking aid, let me urge you first to come to Lampedusa and see these people face to face."

It's natural to feel uncomfortable looking at our own flaws in the mirror, but sometimes by looking at someone else's reflection, we can see ourselves more clearly.

Shrugging off the plight of others makes us nothing more than traffickers in human misery.

So let's stop shifting the blame onto God or drug dealers or poor people. Let's stop blaming the victims. And let's accept our responsibility to alleviate the immense suffering at our borders.

Make Jesus Semitic Again

Mormons have a long, troubled history of racism, well documented in Joanna Brooks' *Mormonism and White Supremacy*. Feeble attempts at addressing the problem consisted mostly of changing the wording in a few Book of Mormon passages from "white and delightsome" to "pure and delightsome." But numerous systemic problems must be addressed for the LDS Church to make any meaningful progress toward a racially equitable culture, and one essential step is to convert Nordic Jesus back to Semitic Jesus.

Mormon officials tell us they don't constrain the imagination of the artists they commission. It's not *their* fault that almost all depictions of Joseph Smith translating the gold plates show viewers… the gold plates. Witness accounts, of course, describe Joseph translating the Book of Mormon by putting his face into a hat and dictating the words that appeared before him, the plates themselves nowhere in sight. Whether or not Church leaders are instructing Mormon artists to depict Jesus Christ as European, and an increasingly light-haired one at that, they are fully capable of asking artists to instead depict Jesus as a Semitic man.

If Church leaders are afraid the majority of white members won't be able to identify with a Savior who doesn't look like them, can we ask why they don't worry about non-white members having this same reaction to Nordic Jesus?

Snarkier critics might even ask why one or more of the apostles can't simply hire a top-notch forensic artist and give a personal description of the Savior. This police sketch artist could develop a basic image from an eyewitness account that could then be handed over to a more artistic painter to create a final, Church-approved product.

If the Quorum of the Twelve defer, saying it's better that the membership not know exactly what Jesus looks like, perhaps they could commission a variety of Jesuses. We can still have Nordic Jesus for Mormons unable to worship a Semitic Jesus. We can have a Semitic Jesus for those who are comfortable with reasonable historical accuracy. We could have a Native American Jesus, an African Jesus, an Asian Jesus, a Polynesian Jesus, an Indian Jesus, and assorted others so that the worldwide membership we profess could all enjoy a Jesus of their own ethnicity.

While we're at it, we might want to rethink the European "Nephite" Moroni on top of every LDS temple.

Removing a statue of a white supremacist to a museum, whether a political, religious, or educational leader, isn't "destroying" or "falsifying" history. Renaming a building or university that is currently named after a racist isn't destroying our religion. We can still read all about these folks as much as we want.

At least as much as the Church itself will allow. Church leaders and their correlation committees already have a 200-year history of hiding uncomfortable information. But if we must try out names of real people, let's consider Fawn Brodie, Helmuth Hubener, Jane Manning, Elijah Abel, George Romney, Wallace Stegner, Arnold Friberg, Gladys Knight, Carol Lynn Pearson, Moroni Olsen, and Hugh Nibley.

What are some names of leaders among the Ute, Paiute, Shoshone, Goshute, and Navajo?

How about names of Mormon suffragettes?

If all of this is simply too overwhelming, if it's easier to just ask non-white members to put up with our white-centric culture, the least we can do is become more transparent about it. If we can't start painting a Semitic Jesus, we can at least change the name of a hymn or two. Let's start with "A Poor, Wayfaring Man of European Descent."

Beheading Rats, Harassing Women, and Making Artificial Cerebrospinal Fluid

"Catch that rat!" Dr. Glickman reached for the terrified white rat scampering across the counter in his Physiology lab. "Damn, Hamid, I told you to be careful when using the ether!"

Hamid didn't seem particularly concerned but quickly caught the rat by trapping it with a trash can. He dabbed an extra bit of ether on a ball of cotton and the rat was soon ready for the guillotine.

"We kill these rats to do our research," Dr. Glickman went on, "but we can still treat them humanely while they're alive. There's no need to terrorize them."

I was interning in the professor's lab for a semester to put something interesting on my medical school application. Assisting in hypoxia experiments was the general description of the work, but my individual tasks included monitoring and reviewing long sheets of readouts, making electrodes out of thin glass tubes, spinning brain matter in a centrifuge, and carefully measuring out ingredients to make up batches of artificial cerebrospinal fluid.

One of the more unnerving assignments was to reach deep into a cylinder of liquid nitrogen to freeze samples. With all the fog generated upon opening the cylinder, there was no way to tell how close my hand was to the liquid.

Also unnerving was running the spectrometer. When I finished, if I didn't flush the blue liquid I used during my analysis, it would stain the tubing. I'd already been chastised once for it.

I didn't even want to be a physician. Not really. But after a BA in English, an MA and an MFA, and a year toward my doctorate, I realized I had no desire to spend the rest of my life writing academic literary criticism. And teaching involved a constant series of complaints. I was either too hard or too easy. I consistently ranked low in "Returns exams to students promptly." Yet I always returned them the very next class period.

So what *could* I do that might feel more valuable? My partner's HIV had just developed into full-blown AIDS. I wanted, at the very least, to be able to understand relevant medical literature. Since it appeared the left side of my brain worked well enough, perhaps the right side would, too. I enrolled at the University of New Orleans again to begin a new degree, this time in Biology. Of course, I hadn't had a single math class in over fifteen years, so God only knew how it would all turn out.

Back in my suburban middle school just outside the city, I had somehow found myself following an "advanced" scholastic tract, taking Algebra I in 8th grade. I say "taking" and not "learning" because I ended up with a D for the course. In Honors English, my teacher called me "Silly dumb!" in front of the class. (Yes, Ms. Hayes, students remember things like that.) Still, I liked school most of the time, except for the bullies. I hadn't meant to whack Ms. Seiler the last day of class. I'd been aiming for Carl.

That same year, my sister, a year older than I was, pissed off some Mean Girls in her public high school, and my parents rushed to find a private school they could afford. My sister ended up in a tiny Pre-K through 12th grade Baptist school a mile from David Duke's home in Metairie. The following year, I entered 9th grade at the same private school, and one of my new friends couldn't stop expressing his admiration for the Grand Wizard.

The entire 9th grade consisted of only thirty students, and now, instead of being the dumbest kid in Honors class, I was among the top students without even trying. I took Algebra I again and made an A. I still can't say I truly learned it, though. When the school chose me to compete with other algebra students across the region, I came nowhere near placing.

In 10th grade, I learned geometry. Yes, learned. Using theorems to solve problems was fun.

In 11th grade, I took a Physics course. The teacher sat at his desk every day studying for his own classes at the Baptist seminary across town in Gentilly, while I and the other students pretended to learn without his help. We didn't. An exchange student from Brazil sat next to me, appalled at American education.

12th grade wasn't much better. In the nine months we studied Algebra II, we only made it through two chapters of the textbook. A classmate of mine—a young man who later became a Seventh-day Adventist pastor—would raise his hand and say, "I don't get it," as soon as the teacher finished each section of a chapter. The teacher, daughter of the school's preacher, would nod patiently and start to go over the concept again. My classmate would then turn to the rest of us and grin at his success.

Yet somehow, when I took my ACT, I scored high enough that when I started college the following year, I was exempted from taking any math courses. I made it through the next three and a half degrees without so much as multiplying a fraction.

So once I decided on a Biology degree, I signed up for two remedial math courses and then plowed ahead with trigonometry, physics, and chemistry. Organic Chemistry was more fun, though, a puzzle like the geometry had been. Genetics was enjoyable, too, though I found it challenging to meet with my professor after every single exam and explain to him why the answer he'd subtracted ten points from was in fact 100% correct. Each time, he'd review my test and say, "Oh, yeah, you're right. Sorry about that."

Another semester, I made an appointment to talk with my Chemistry II professor in his office. "Dr. Pearce," I said, "I've done this problem over and over and keep getting the same answer, but it doesn't match the answer in the back of the book. I don't understand my mistake."

"That's because the book's wrong," he said. "You did it right."

I was astounded. How could the publisher not fix the error? Why did the professor not warn us?

And how in the world had I become good at this?

I was not a challenger by nature but being an adjunct instructor while studying helped. Just a mile down the road was Southern University, a historically Black public institution, still segregated forty years after *Brown v. Board of Education.* Of course, what my own students challenged *me* about was my racism, which I wasn't even aware I had.

Eventually, I was a senior once again, with only a few courses left before earning my BS. My GPA was 3.75 and I'd scored 27 on my MCAT both times I'd taken it, not great but good enough. I just needed something a little more interesting to add to my application. Beheading rats might be the thing.

Unfortunately, life in the Physiology lab wasn't very pleasant. Dr. Glickman was great, generally kind and patient. He'd gone out of his way to hire Hamid, whose parents had immigrated from Palestine. He had no idea Hamid made fun of him when he left the lab.

"*Schindler's List* was on TV last night," he told me one day, releasing the weight pulling on a heated glass tube.

"Yes," I said carefully, "I watched it."

"Did you cry?" Hamid made an exaggerated expression of melodramatic unhappiness. Then his lip turned up in disgust. "Jews always talk about the Holocaust," he went on, "but they do the same thing to Palestinians."

Another day, he boasted about his sexual conquests. "Jewish girls love me to fuck them," he said. "Makes them feel open-minded."

Raised Mormon in a Catholic city with Baptist relatives on a Mississippi dairy farm, I knew almost nothing about Palestinians. Two years as a Mormon missionary in Rome hadn't done anything to alter that. But after I was excommunicated for being gay, I eventually learned more about Judaism when I became partnered with a Reform Jew. Then, after a year of Intro to Judaism with the rabbi before Torah Study, I officially converted.

But I still didn't learn much about Palestinians.

When Hamid had an accident on his skateboard and ended up in the hospital with a collapsed lung, I went to visit him. My partner insisted on coming along, also insisting on wearing his yarmulke. Hamid's mother was by her son's bedside when we entered his room. Upon seeing my partner's kipa, she said, very calmly but firmly, "As Jews, you must understand how important it is to have a homeland."

My partner, who regularly complained in private about Palestinians, or Muslims of any ethnicity, smiled politely and agreed with Hamid's mother. He and I remained friends for several years after breaking up, but his constant rants against Muslims ultimately forced me to break off even friendship.

At the time I worked with Hamid, then, I could only see the negative. And there was plenty of it. When a female Chinese student began working part-time in the lab, Hamid would try to engage her in talking about Communism, even after she made it clear she was afraid she was being monitored and that officials back in Beijing would find out anything she said which might be interpreted as negative. Instead, she'd leave the room when he brought up the subject again and again. Another day, he pulled up a recording of the fake orgasm scene from *When Harry Met Sally*, playing it over and over until the young woman fled the lab.

"Oh, it's so fun to tease her," Hamid told me, laughing.

He was a paid lab assistant. I was only an unpaid, part-time intern, and a wuss at that, but I did manage to say, "Let's hope she doesn't charge you with sexual harassment."

"What?" Hamid laughed. "That wasn't harassment! I'm just having a little fun!"

I don't remember much else about the time I spent in the Physiology lab. Once, Hamid made a comment expressing his confidence Dr. Glickman would never fire him because he'd feel too guilty, but that was about it.

I applied to medical school six years in a row, interviewing five times, but I was never accepted. The last year I interviewed, the dean said, "I have no problem with your academics. I just don't think you have the right personality to be a physician."

I got a job checking out books at the New Orleans Public Library, which paid better than anything I'd earned the ten years I taught English. I lost my job and apartment when Hurricane Katrina hit, relocating to Seattle, where I began working at a payday loan office, preying on the homeless, near homeless, and the desperate day after day. After moving up the ladder to work as a teller at a credit union (which was far more like a bank than they wanted to admit) and then on to a mortgage department to process equity loans, I discovered I didn't have the right personality for any of those, either.

I remember in high school taking a job aptitude assessment, amused that the dot on the resultant graph was far from *any* career the exam was testing for. Turns out I'm a writer, and not many people make a living at that.

After my husband joined the Freedom Socialist Party, I learned leftist (often Jewish leftist) political theory, and I *finally* learned more about Palestinians. I'm struck that so many Americans vigorously support Israel no matter how its government treats "minorities" within its own borders. Israeli leaders couldn't even muster enough of a sense of community to avoid "othering" Ethiopian Jewish refugees, instead deliberately creating policies to prevent their full integration into society.

I haven't spoken to Hamid in twenty years and have no desire to look him up. I expect he's still not the kind of guy I'd want to hang out with. But I understand at least a little better where he's coming from, and I understand that no one (not African Americans, not Native Americans, not atheists, not LGBTQ folks, not women, not Palestinians, not *anyone*) needs to be "nice" to deserve the complete, full allotment of human rights.

I do miss making artificial cerebrospinal fluid, though. Who knew that such a vital substance could be so simple?

Now, if only we could learn to splice the empathy gene into a strand of DNA, avoid the dangers of eugenics, and ask for a few volunteers…

Of course, we'd already need to have empathy to conduct any such procedure in an ethical, safe way, and humanity is nowhere near being capable of that.

For now, then, I keep searching for a way to tell stories that help develop deeper understanding and promote better behavior, in the hope that the one job I am qualified for might still eventually offer value.

Sex Is Work

When I mentioned to my Book Club friends that I'd once worked as an escort, one woman, after quizzing me several minutes, asked her final, horrified question, "So you had *sex* with these people?"

Despite the obvious answer, she couldn't wrap her head around such a concept. But she's not the only one. *I'm* biased, too. The stigma is so great that despite years working in various parts of the sex industry, I too find myself constantly battling an internalized bias.

Watching a scene in *La Porta Rossa* in which a detective questions a female dancer at a strip club in Trieste, I said to my husband, "I went to a gay strip club like that on Times Square, where you could sit behind glass and watch a guy take a shower." But while my words might have been neutral, my tone carried a hint of disdain.

Was I, after all my experiences with various parts of the sex industry, really going to judge?

Growing up Mormon, I was taught that a woman wearing a sleeveless dress was "breaking the Law of Chastity." Sundresses aren't girl-next-door attire. They're what sex-crazed sluts wear.

When Seattle established a streetcar line in the South Lake Union business district, developers labeled it the South Lake Union Transit.

S.L.U.T.

What were they thinking? When a friend invited us to a Mardi Gras party, my husband slapped together a cardboard streetcar, taped it to a hat, and scribbled SLUT in black marker on his T-shirt to attend the party.

I went dressed as myself, since I was already a slut.

Back in New Orleans for full-fledged Mardi Gras celebrations, I threw beads from the balconies of gay bars, bribing men with the plastic treasures in exchange for showing their dicks.

Most of my sluttiness occurred on other days of the year—fucking strangers in bathhouses, participating in sex parties at a private club, groping and being groped in the darkened upstairs room of a neighborhood levi/leather bar.

But all of that sex was "free" and so not tainted in the eyes of many of my gay friends, who did as much or more than I ever did but would never "lower" themselves to either charge or pay.

As a missionary in Italy, I saw a beautiful teenage girl one afternoon on a commuter train heading for Frascati, just outside Rome. Worried some creepy guy would pressure her for sex, I handed her a pamphlet on the importance of sexual purity.

In Naples, my companion and I caught a bus across from Ospedale Cardarelli to go home for the evening. Just a few feet away was a campfire where several female prostitutes worked. "You know what they say," my companion quipped one evening. "You should enjoy your work."

Even while fantasizing about sex with men, I was judging the sex lives of others.

I remained a virgin until I was twenty-six, but when I finally accepted my sexual and affectional orientation, I reexamined all my sexual attitudes. Were one-night stands OK? Was it OK to date two men at the same time? To pick someone up at a bus stop?

To spend the night with a DJ working the graveyard shift at a classical music station?

I ultimately decided that pretty much anything consenting adults agreed to was OK, as long as the participants were honest. If you wanted an open relationship and all parties agreed to it, great. If you simply *said* you were in an open relationship but were really cheating, that wasn't cool at all.

Granted, I still felt uncomfortable when I stopped by a guy's house for a date and he introduced me to his wife before we headed off to the movies. "I'll have your husband home by 10:00," I promised.

It wasn't until one of my freshman college students wrote a paper on why he thought prostitution should be legalized that I reconsidered my position on that "obviously" unacceptable behavior. The points I remember most were those focusing on the safety of both the customers *and* the sex workers, but there were a good many other persuasive points as well.

I gave the student an A, not because his paper was perfect, but because it did the only thing a successful argument can do—make someone reevaluate their position, whatever their ultimate conclusion.

Over the years, I became friends with escorts, even dated an escort, and saw that my judgment had been as misguided as the judgment my former Mormon friends harbored about LGBTQ folks.

I escorted for about eighteen months in my early forties and discovered that most of the men who hired me were normal, decent guys.

Now, I realize this isn't the case with folks who coerce others into the sex trade. Trafficking or taking advantage of runaways or people with addiction is another subject altogether. It would be like a dairy producing milk for vanilla ice cream being compared to a company adding melamine to its baby formula. It's the difference between medicine and snake oil, between selling music and selling pirated music, between running for office to serve your constituents or running to serve yourself.

Sex work, whether that's via books, magazines, films, toys, or bodies, should be compared to services addressing other basic needs.

Is it immoral to make money selling or preparing food? Are cookbooks and cooking shows sinful? Ovens and cookware? Farmers' markets? Food is a fundamental human need, but no one sees commercializing it as beyond the pale.

Without sleep, humans suffer mental breakdown and death. But who's arguing that selling mattresses or hammocks or sleeping bags is the work of the Devil?

Every human being produces human waste. But do we consider companies and workers providing toilets and toilet paper and plumbing and sewers underworld criminals?

Humans also need shelter, so architects and contractors create housing at various prices. As a society, while we complain about the high cost of housing, we also look down on anyone who can't afford it. It doesn't occur to the average American that charging for this basic necessity is a sin.

So we all routinely accept that bodily needs such as food, housing, sleep, and waste can only be served by monetizing them.

But sex? *That's* unacceptable.

My first boyfriend was born with visible physical differences many people found unappealing and as a result frequently hired sex workers. He had normal sexual needs and not many men were interested in "volunteering" their services.

They should have been—he was quite good at it.

Old people, heavy people, folks with features not deemed attractive by others, and people with various mental health issues almost all have sexual needs, whether or not anyone is sexually attracted to them. Our society makes anyone not fitting very narrow norms into sexual outcasts. I've had sex with many of these folks, though, and most encounters were as enjoyable as those with folks who possessed more traditionally acceptable bodies.

And some weren't fun at all. But I've never felt like I was selling my soul more than when as a cashier in retail I had to put up with the vilest customers imaginable. I couldn't tell the jerks what I thought of them without getting fired. I needed the money, so I put up with a lot of crap from customers, coworkers, and employers.

Why is it morally acceptable to put up with abuse and humiliation "at the office" but a terrible moral failing to voluntarily agree to someone's non-abusive, non-humiliating sexual request?

I once did temp work installing attic insulation, a job far more physically abusive than even the kinkiest sex, paid or unpaid, I ever engaged in.

A teacher hired me once as a treat during a "mental health day" absence from work.

Some guys got together and hired me as a birthday present for a friend.

I serviced a trucker, a busy executive, and a variety of other men. Sometimes, I'd walk into a five-star hotel and head straight for the elevator and up to the room number I'd been given. Other times, I'd walk down Canal Street at 1:00 in the morning past the Iberville projects, afraid I was going to be mugged or killed.

But I needed the money. I'd maxed out my student loans and still had a few courses left to complete.

And no sex assignment terrified me as much as the night I brought home a guy who had targeted me at a bar because I was friends with his boyfriend, who he beat regularly.

That moment when I was naked in bed, completely vulnerable, and he revealed who he was and why he was there, is one I'll never forget.

As an escort, I only refused to have sex with a single client. His behavior was so obnoxious that even though I'd initially agreed to go to his hotel, once it was time to conduct business, I told him I'd changed my mind and walked off.

That was unpleasant, but I left with my soul intact, something I can't say about the many "acceptable" jobs I've had which forced me to put up with poor behavior day after day after day.

Sex work, already legal in some places, should be legalized everywhere, to make work servicing this basic human need safer for all involved.

Of course, workers in *all* fields need more support, recognition, and protections. We saw during the pandemic that "essential" workers were also those most often placed in dangerous environments with little recourse to protect themselves and few resources if they were sickened or injured.

Sex work isn't valued in society because the bulk of it is seen as "women's work," which is traditionally undervalued. But it's as essential as childcare, as housecleaning, as teaching, as nursing.

Criminalizing it is like criminalizing the food court at the mall or making it a crime to post recipes online.

Can you imagine being arrested for flushing your toilet? For buying a new mattress? (Or tearing the tag off it?)

We have so many urgent needs in society—universal healthcare, tuition-free college and vocational training, and immediate transition away from fossil fuels—that it's easy to forget sex is a "real" need, too.

I hope we can make an effort to reduce our moralizing and concentrate more on addressing universal human needs, even if it's something as distasteful as selling toilet brushes or coming up with a new flavor for lube.

Trick-or-Treating with the Homeless

"What's going on outside?" asked The Magician. "Is there a festival today?"

I called him The Magician because he'd once recommended the paranormal show to me. He was young, probably late thirties, and quite hot, but I wasn't young, and I wasn't hot, so I satisfied myself with chatting. "I don't know," I said, glancing into the cubbyhole behind the counter, where a TV monitor showed me views from five security cameras. I'd watched a SWAT team raid an illegal hookah lounge next door on those cameras. I'd watched as a vacant building behind us was ravaged by an arsonist.

"Looks like trick-or-treaters," I said. A few young children in costumes walked past the front of the adult video store. Thankfully, some of the kids were accompanied by their parents. How awkward it might be if any of the kids ventured inside. Hopefully, they'd pass by the massage parlor down the block, too.

The Magician stepped back as another of our regulars came to the counter. "Could you change the movie in the straight theater?" he asked. "I've seen that one already." Months ago, I'd asked the man the ethnic origin of his name, and he'd told me he was Kurdish, born in the U.S. after his parents immigrated here forty years earlier. I chose not to bring up the latest political betrayal that was already fading from the news as other outrageous decisions took its place.

I switched out the movie and turned back to The Magician. He was from Ohio and commented on the difficulty of making friends here in Seattle. "People are polite," he said, "but they're not really friendly. It's like someone sitting on their front porch, waving you over for a glass of tea, but no matter how many times they invite you onto the porch, they never let you inside the house."

I smiled, thinking of the times we'd enjoyed long chats comparing the new *Charmed* with the old one, or whether *The Librarians* was as good as his favorite show. And how every time we had one of these chats, there would inevitably come a moment when a distinctive look appeared on The Magician's face as he began to worry my friendliness was all a ruse so I could proposition him.

A tall, striking middle-aged man walked into the store and headed for the arcade. The Magician's eyes lit up, and I nodded for him to go check him out.

Soon, it was 4:00 and time for shift change. I counted my till, just finishing as the evening guy came in. I'd watched the security footage of young men from the hookah lounge accosting Aaron after work one evening as he left through the rear door at midnight. They tried to force him underneath the stairs in the alley. I could see him stop when he reached the last giant trash bin, which offered him a chance to squeeze past the blockade. He instinctively knew not to give up that last opportunity for escape.

The guys taunted and threatened him, but he remained calm. Then finally, the leader tapped Aaron on the shoulder and let him leave. I'd shivered when I saw that, recognizing just how serious the situation had been.

"Excellent!" I said. "I'm balanced!" I signed out and moved aside to let him sign in. Though we'd been coworkers for three years, our shifts only overlapped a few minutes a day, so it wasn't until I ran into him at a Net Neutrality protest that we started to bond. He was having some financial troubles now, and I tried to leave him a protein shake or some other treat for his evening shifts.

As I headed toward the door, an attractive Asian man who'd just entered, one of our regulars, wished me a good evening. Straight guys were often nervous around gay men, but this man was always pleasant to me.

Out on the sidewalk, I immediately had to step past a homeless man bundled under a sleeping bag in front of the vacant store next door. I watched as three young trick-or-treaters did the same. One of the boys was Spiderman. Another was a warrior. The girl wore the horn of a unicorn.

I continued to the bus stop, passing a wine and beer store where I could see several children in costumes milling about with their parents. I crossed the street and passed a Thai restaurant and a boxing ring. Next to that was a pot shop, H&R Block, and a pawn shop. More trick-or-treaters walked by, one small group accompanied by someone's father dressed as a dinosaur.

All the trick-or-treaters looked white and middle class.

A short, dirty man rummaged through a trash can. "Do you have any change?" he asked me.

I looked him in the eye, not willing for him to be the Invisible Man, but declined his offer. "You have a good day," he said with a nod. I wondered if he was trying to guilt trip me.

If he was, it was working.

I passed a vinyl record store, a business offering boudoir photos, and then a coffeeshop, where one of the workers sat out front with a huge bowl of candy. She handed a few pieces to the children passing by. I continued past Proletariat Pizza and a gay bar called Swallow. Another gay bar, along with a straight bar, sat across the street, next to a tattoo parlor and a jiu jitsu academy. I watched as a tiny princess and a boy dressed as a dog walked toward a roller girl rink just past them.

I popped into a smoke shop to buy a lottery ticket, followed in by a mother with two costumed children. The cashier offered them treats from a large bowl.

I walked past one more homeless man sitting under a blanket and smoking. He looked at me and I looked back, but neither of us said anything.

Finally, as I approached the corner, only a block now from the bus stop, I saw a young woman dressed as a witch, sitting on a stool in front of a newly opened eatery, with a large bowl of candy on her lap. "This isn't the kind of trick-or-treating I did as a child," I said to her in passing. "These kids are getting quite a different cultural experience."

She nodded. "A couple of the homeless guys cried when I gave them some candy," she told me.

It seemed unlikely, but she had no reason to lie.

"Do you want some?" She held the bowl out for me.

"Oh, no thanks. I'm diabetic anyway."

"Would you like a sticker?" She offered me a jack-o'-lantern to put on my shirt.

Inclusive. And yet I couldn't quite decide if I was experiencing something truly positive or not. On the one hand, kids weren't being kept in a bubble. They were seeing the "real" world. On the other, they seemed to be polishing a technique not often mastered until adulthood—ignoring the suffering of those right in front of them, in order to get what they wanted.

"We have to look out for the most vulnerable members of our society," the witch told me with deep sincerity.

Because two pieces of candy would do that.

I smiled anyway, because it *was* more than most people did, and I wished her well, continuing past a store selling Mexican convenience food. I'd stopped in once, but everything I could afford consisted solely of carbs and fat. At the bus stop across from the gas station, an ancient Asian woman shuffled toward the bench, where she sat next to a heavyset white woman in her fifties, her hair colored blue and purple, smoking a cigarette.

The middle-aged woman had no teeth.

I wished I remembered The Magician's name.

At least my husband had invited me inside from the porch. We'd recently celebrated twelve years together. Tonight after dinner, we planned to watch the last episode of *Spirited*, a quirky Australian show about a dentist in love with the ghost of a dead rock star.

The elderly Asian woman struggled to stand up. The 60 had just rounded the corner. The blue-haired woman stood behind her as the driver opened the doors. After waiting for them to board, I climbed up as well.

Do We See the Person in "Homeless Person"?

I work in a seedy part of town. When I get off the bus in the morning, I walk two blocks in the darkness past abandoned stores, closed massage parlors and bars, and ethnic eateries that won't be open for hours.

About fifteen or twenty homeless folks are huddled under blankets or umbrellas, some blocking themselves off with shopping carts to protect them as they sleep.

They aren't all asleep, though, not even with sunrise still an hour away. Even so, the homeless men I pass on my way to work don't frighten me as much as the guys walking around who *aren't* homeless, who are out doing some kind of personal "business" at this ungodly hour.

The store where I work caters to an eclectic clientele. Businessmen, construction workers, accountants, professors—lots of different folks come in every day. Including a few homeless guys and some others who are not far from it.

A few days ago, a man robbed a pizza place next door, slapping and roughing up the young woman on duty. Over the past couple of years I've been working in the neighborhood, two men have been killed a few feet from our front door, after hours, the result of conflicts at the bar across the street. Another morning when I arrived to open up, I discovered police investigating the shooting of three people in the alley behind our business.

When homeless or borderline homeless folks come into the store, my own biases click in, and I'm on the alert for shoplifting. Theft is a constant battle at our location anyway. I've learned which of our "regular" homeless visitors must be asked to leave the moment they walk in and which are usually respectful enough to be left to themselves, even if they are unlikely to buy anything. One man, around thirty, with decent income and not homeless, likes to shoplift for the "thrill." He explained that he pretends to break into cars sometimes, too, just for the excitement of being caught or chased.

If "it takes a village," part of that village must include mental health counseling.

One semi-regular, his hands always a bit dirty, wearing clothes that aren't quite clean, with a "rough" look to his demeanor, has been in my "undecided" category for a while. I'm never quite sure about him, but so far, he hasn't seemed to cause any trouble.

The other day, he surprised me.

"You've lost some weight, haven't you?" he asked when he came to the register to conduct a small transaction. "You look good." He nodded approvingly.

Diabetic and overweight, I've been struggling for a long while to get in better shape and have finally started losing a few of those deadly pounds. My husband's noticed but no one else has. Except this homeless or borderline homeless man.

He's come in the store for a year now, and I still don't know his name.

A compliment doesn't change his financial situation, or the level of risk he may or may not pose to our inventory, but it does remind me that all these scary people I see every day on my way to work, or even *at* work, are still human beings. Flawed, perhaps, but who isn't? As much as it might comfort us to believe otherwise, not all homeless, nearly homeless, or marginally employed people end up in their desperate situations because they're "bad."

Short of a complete overhaul of our political and economic systems, there may be little we can do personally to make life better for some of the destitute folks we see every day. But if we can do just one thing—acknowledge their humanity—they can more easily remember they're human beings and not the trash society has told them they are.

It's OK to look people in the eye. It's OK even to be a little scared. But, surely, the very least we can do is notice them.

LGBTQ Lit for Mormons

A Mormon missionary in Italy abandons his mission to move in with the Italian man he loves. A conflicted Mormon father is confronted with a transgender son who wants to be his daughter. A polygamist in 1855 Utah is ordered to take a fourth wife, when all he really wants is to be with another man. A virginal gay man takes out a contract on his own life to protect his virtue.

If I could have read stories like these before my mission, perhaps I wouldn't have stood at the railing of a ferry taking me from Sardinia to the mainland of Italy, staring at the water for two hours as I contemplated suicide. "The weather is so nasty," I thought. "No one else is on deck. Everyone would think I'd slipped in the storm."

Because of my Church's extreme homophobia, this course of action actually seemed like the best option for me. A gay convert I was assigned to Home Teach years later did deliberately overdose on pills. As did a family friend whose father told him, "I'd rather hear my son was dead than that he was gay." If stories about LGBTQ Mormons were routinely available to young members of the Church, perhaps the suicide rate for LGBTQ teens in Utah wouldn't be one of the highest in the nation.

Unless we'd rather hear about those high death rates than about our LGBTQ youth coming out.

Of over 425 short stories I've published in thirty books, almost half of them deal with gay Mormons. My books include *Mormon Underwear*, *Sex Among the Saints*, *Gayrabian Nights*, and many more. Six of my books have been named to Kirkus Reviews' Best of the Year.

And I'm not alone in writing about the gay Mormon experience. Marty Beaudet writes about a gay missionary in Europe recruited by his mission president to work for the CIA. Ryan Rhodes describes the horror of electroshock torture at BYU. Writer Jeff Laver addresses various aspects of the gay Mormon world as well. Brian Andersen produces a comic book about a gay Mormon superhero called *Stripling Warrior*.

Heterosexual Mormons write about LGBTQ members, too—Donna Banta, Eric Samuelsen, Levi Peterson, Mette Ivie Harrison, and the esteemed Carol Lynn Pearson. An anthology of some of the best work about LGBTQ Mormons, *Latter-Gay Saints*, is edited by Gerald Argetsinger, former Artistic Director of the Hill Cumorah Pageant.

The truth is that Mormons should support *all* LDS art and literature more fully. And this means reading work other than that published solely by Deseret Book. Intellectual and progressive Mormons enjoy reading history and non-fiction, but facts alone tell a mere fraction of the story. It is the lived experience illustrated in various forms of literature that reveal the most to us. It's the difference between reading a scholarly article on the Holocaust versus watching *Schindler's List.*

As most Mormons know, the LDS Church is frequently in the national news because of its homophobic policies. It raised twenty million dollars for Prop 8 and has worked tirelessly behind the scenes to fight same-sex marriage since the early 1990s. In 2015, the LDS Church redefined apostasy to include same-sex marriage. And it implemented a new policy denying its ordinances and blessings to children of same-sex couples.

Mormons make up a powerful voting bloc in the western U.S., and those voters often, in the most well-meaning of ways, deliberately hurt their own LGBTQ family members. The worst part is that they sincerely believe they're demonstrating love by doing so.

But well-intentioned Mormons only keep hurting us because they don't really know us on a deeper level. Fortunately, there are groups such as the Mama Dragons, Q-Saints, and Family Fellowship who help LGBTQ Mormons and their allies support each other.

But all Mormons could make a stronger effort to understand gay, lesbian, bisexual, transgender, and asexual people more fully, both in and out of the Church. Certainly, those who consider themselves our allies need to do so. One easy and effective way to accomplish this is through reading work by gay Mormon artists trying to humanize those so often demonized by religion.

Yes, there are some four-letter words among our pages, and there might even be an allusion or two to sex. But if we're not strong enough to read about real life without swooning, we're not going to be much help to the LGBTQ friends and family we claim to love.

True understanding can only come about if we make the effort. Let's read what our LGBTQ brothers and sisters write to know more about their world.

More Social Justice, Less Civil Disorder

An acquaintance of mine complained that her friend's small business had been destroyed by all the recent protests for racial justice. Her friend's store had not been physically damaged, mind you. It was simply located in an area where a great deal of protesting took place. The owner had been forced to board up her windows, and the few customers she'd managed to hang onto during the pandemic disappeared. "Who do these protesters think they're helping?" my friend asked in disgust. "They're hurting innocent people!"

A gunman with his weapon aimed at the head of a hostage will warn the police officer approaching, "Take another step and I'll kill her. Her death will be *your* fault. *You're* killing her."

Abusers often blame their victims for the abuse. "You *made* me hit you! This is *your* fault!"

But the abuser is responsible for abusing. The killer is responsible for killing.

If people don't want protests against police brutality, they are free to demand police accountability. If people don't like political unrest, they are free to work for social justice.

Yes, small businesses *are* suffering terribly during the pandemic. No debate there. But that's not the fault of the citizens being legally murdered or those who care about them. When politicians give the ultra-wealthy hundreds of billions of dollars during an economic crisis *instead* of assisting workers and small businesses, it's the oppressors who are to blame, no matter how we might personally feel about the targets of the oppression.

Even if you have legitimate reason to hate hornets, if you hit their nest with a stick again and again, you'd be a fool not to expect them to react. And when we're talking about other human beings facing inhumane treatment at the hands of other humans, it's intellectually dishonest to pretend we expect anything other than rage.

A Mormon friend of mine becomes defensive any time the subject of race comes up. "Whites didn't start the slave trade," he says. "Black people in Africa started selling their own people to whites. Why is that *our* fault? We just took what we were being offered. Anyone would do that. But *we're* the ones who have to take all the blame. If white Americans hadn't bought their slaves, someone else would."

He didn't seem aware that at least ten million Africans were sold to eager slaveowners in other countries.

But he was also oblivious to the most glaring problem with his justification. "If a man kidnapped your daughter," I said, "and sold her into the sex trade, you'd blame the kidnapper, wouldn't you?"

"Of course. Scumbags like that should be executed."

"But you'd give a pass to every man who paid your daughter's owner to rape her? You'd feel that if *those* particular men didn't rape her, other men would, so there'd be no point holding the men who did rape your daughter accountable?"

"It's not the same thing. And I certainly wouldn't hold the great-great-grandchildren of the rapists accountable."

"But would you acknowledge that their great-great-grandrapist did do something inexcusable? Would you hold the great-great-grandchildren of the kidnapper responsible *to any degree at all* for sharing some of the wealth *they* accumulated through the kidnapping? Wealth that had time to multiply a hundred-fold, a thousand-fold, in all the years since? If it's OK for the innocent great-great-grandchildren of kidnappers to benefit from crimes they didn't commit, why is it bad for the great-great-grandchildren of the victims to receive any kind of reparation for those crimes?"

Even working-class white people today still benefit financially from the kidnapping, rape, torture, enslavement, and murder of Africans, whether or not our individual ancestors ever owned slaves. Slave traders and slave owners created a culture that continues to benefit us, whether we want to benefit or not, whether or not we still experience financial struggles.

Our justice system is structurally racist. Our education system, too. So is the film industry, journalism, and healthcare. But the institution causing most of our inequality is capitalism, which can't function without it.

Our many failures cannot be corrected without simultaneously addressing the racism built into almost all of our institutions. Focusing on one at a time is a bit like untying a kidnap victim's left leg but leaving all other bindings intact. Even if we eventually untie her completely but leave her in a locked room, she's still not really free.

Remember the three young women kidnapped and imprisoned for years in a house in Cleveland? A fund was established to help them move on from a decade of captivity and rape. By itself, walking out the door of that hellhole wasn't enough to give them more than the slimmest chance at recovery. They needed financial assistance, even if those funds were provided by people who bore no personal responsibility for the crimes committed. The descendants of African slaves *might* be content just to be released, only we've made sure they can never fully be free. At the very least, reparations must include dismantling the structures that originally caused and still perpetuate their suffering.

Our systems aren't "broken." They were designed this way.

In Philadelphia, eleven non-violent men, women, and children were burned to death in their home by the police… for protesting police brutality.

In Louisville, a sleeping woman working on the pandemic's front line was "legally" shot to death in her own bed.

In a classic horror film, Carol Kane learns to her dismay, "The call is coming from inside the house!"

If my friend's daughter really were to be kidnapped, how would he feel if at some point, in an attempt to escape, she killed a man who was raping her? Perhaps the man having sex with the kidnapped girl believed he was engaged in a consensual act. Maybe *he* thought he was innocent.

I'd say no one in their right mind would fault the young woman for killing an "innocent" man in order to save herself, but then, we all know what happened to Cyntoia Brown. And Chrystul Kizer. And Sarah Kruzan. If the "perpetrator" is black, her color is the crime, not the atrocities being committed against her.

It's possible—indeed unavoidable—to be imperfect and still be the primary victim in an encounter, on either an individual or institutional level. If "both sides" bear some blame, one side can still bear 97% of it. And, as often as not, the violence and looting taking place these past few weeks have been perpetrated by right-wing folks trying to implicate protesters. Sometimes, police officers themselves can be seen breaking store windows. Occasionally, it's left-wing white people thinking they're doing black folks a favor. But even when it *is* black protesters damaging businesses of "innocent" people, they're still not the real force behind the damage.

Is the kidnapped Abigail Breslin in *The Call* responsible for the death of a would-be rescuer because she followed 9-1-1 dispatcher Halle Berry's advice to attract someone's attention?

White people have found ourselves accessories to both past and present brutality. Perhaps we didn't ask anyone to inflict that brutality. Yet we also feel affinity for some of those committing it and find ourselves reluctant to "betray" our "family" by reporting the abuse and demanding justice. So we choose to wash our hands of the matter. But walking away from the conflict doesn't absolve us of guilt. It simply adds "hit and run" to the list of crimes. The only way to change our complicity is to actively work for justice on the part of those wronged. If small business owners are among those being wronged, the solution is to address the cause, not the *inescapable* consequences of continued oppression.

In the film *The Commuter*, Vera Farmiga plays a character who coerces a man played by Liam Neeson to find a murder witness so that the witness can be killed. Neeson accepts the initial bribe before understanding the full import of the agreement, but then he changes his mind and resists. Each time he refuses to help, though, another innocent person is murdered. "*You* did this!" Vera Farmiga says as Liam watches a longtime friend being pushed in front of a bus.

No. The murderers are Vera and the other criminals she works for. Is Liam *partly* responsible? Yes, he is. He broke "the rules." But no matter what Liam does, Vera and the bad guys are still going to keep killing people. They should be the focus of any animosity. They set everything in motion. They created the structure that ensures all the continued human devastation.

To some extent, even the officer who knocked out the teeth of a Chicago woman, whose only "inappropriate behavior" was shouting at a different officer beating a protester, isn't the real culprit. It's the system that ensures these kinds of abuses will happen again and again no matter how much officials say they'll "try harder" to train their officers to "behave better."

When a police chief in Asheville admits his officers made a mistake by destroying a medical station set up to treat protesters, he misses the larger problem, a structural one—that destroying medical supplies and threatening medical volunteers with tear gas was even one of the possible actions under consideration to begin with.

When we yell at protesters fighting for their financial and physical survival, we're targeting the wrong party. More importantly, doing so won't solve the underlying problems, particularly those of folks struggling to keep their businesses afloat. The institution oppressing both people of color and small businesses is pro-corporate capitalism, which always favors those who have already accumulated wealth on the backs of others. The protester we insist on scapegoating is simply a 911 dispatcher trying to organize emergency assistance to save others from additional kidnapping, rape, and murder.

If we don't like the consequences of either deliberate or accidental oppression, we can't initiate—or perpetuate—the conditions that create them.

That's not simply a better solution than blaming the victim, it's the only one.

Suppression of Information Is a Human Rights Abuse

"You are *not* having sex on that stage!"

"Uh, I didn't know that was an option."

One of the many funny scenes from *Miss Congeniality*, a comedy about a beauty pageant—oh, excuse me—scholarship program. Despite its humor, or perhaps because of it, this bit of dialogue makes an important statement on the human condition—lack of information, especially *withholding* or denying that information, is an act of oppression.

You'd think the Kafkaesque disbelief in the value of wearing face masks during a respiratory pandemic would be impossible to impose on huge swaths of the population. But science-deniers make their decisions on masks and vaccines and climate because of the information they've been given… and the information withheld from them.

In late 1982, my mother began experiencing a heavier than usual period. In January of the following year, she was informed that to stop the bleeding, she'd need a hysterectomy. After a few days recuperating at home, her fever spiked, and she was readmitted to the hospital. The first nurse to visit after she settled in looked at her chart and said cheerily, "Oh, you're the leukemia patient."

My mother turned to my father. "I have leukemia?"

She'd suspected it already. At home, we had a book that provided a list of possible diagnoses for various symptoms. Mom had looked up her bleeding and bruising and whispered to me, "I think I have leukemia."

Even at the age of twenty-one, I understood how hard it was for a lay person to accurately diagnose disease with only two paragraphs of study. But when I went to see my mom in the hospital that January afternoon, she recounted what the nurse had told her, adding, "I finally got the doctor to tell me what kind of leukemia I have, but now he won't give me a prognosis. I need you to go to the library and tell me what you find."

I did and returned the following day with the news. "Well?"

I realized why the doctor hadn't wanted to tell her. "Most people with this form of the disease only live three months."

My mother deflated like a balloon. I didn't have the heart to let her know only a fraction of patients went into remission, and even those who did usually experienced a relapse within a year and never went into remission again.

"They started the chemotherapy without asking me," she said, motioning to the IV in her arm. "If I'd known all this, I would have stayed at home and blown my brains out." She looked angrily toward the door. "But now I'm trapped and can't get out."

When I asked my father why he and the doctor had kept this information from her, he told me they decided she wasn't strong enough emotionally to handle the news, so they'd taken it upon themselves to decide what was best for her. But it was her life, I thought, her misery, her death. She had a right to the most basic information about her own body.

Over the next few weeks, I watched my mother suffer horrifically, covered with bruises from all the needles, lying on a bedpan non-stop, confused, even delirious. "Johnny, you can get your snakes now," she told me one afternoon.

Another time, as a nurse drew blood for the third time that day, she turned to me in disgust and asked, "Why did we join this club?"

On one of the worst days, two nurses struggled for half an hour digging into her arm to insert a rubber tube to make it easier to access her collapsing veins. For *thirty minutes*, my mother cried as the staff tortured her for her own good.

But they finally gave up, unable to get the tube in.

All that suffering for nothing.

When the nurses returned later to inflict more useless pain, Mom looked about the room in confusion, not recognizing me or my grandmother. She threw her arms up to the ceiling and cried out, "I want my mama!"

My grandmother started sobbing.

A few days and a few seizures later, a nurse came in to check on my mom, who was thankfully sleeping. The nurse examined the IV and adjusted it to speed up the flow. But the medicine burned, waking my mother. She reached for the IV, realized she wasn't allowed to touch it, and cried. Her kidneys were now failing. The stress and medication were giving her diabetes.

My father and my mother's doctor, with their privileged information, had decided what was best, three weeks of excruciating misery before Mom's inevitable death. With patriarchy like that, who needs misogyny?

I soon realized this wasn't an isolated case. People are denied vital information every day of their lives. It's not only unethical. It's a violation of human rights.

As a Mormon, I heard my leaders say that homosexuality was an evil choice and that the only way for a gay man to reach heaven was to marry a woman. Coming out under such circumstances was devastating. Many LGBTQ folks in similar situations ended up committing suicide, submitting to electroshock torture, or entering into doomed marriages that damaged even more lives.

My husband's bishop suggested he find a young woman to have sex with. Fornication as therapy, an innocent young woman's body a useful tool.

One of my friends from the Single Adult group magnanimously offered me his girlfriend for practice. "She'll fix your little red wagon."

Ignorance isn't always bliss. Often, it's devastatingly oppressive.

After I came out, I studied homosexuality and the history of religious attitudes, finally understanding what my leaders clearly didn't. I talked to them, wrote letters, gave them reading lists. I'd always been taught—and believed—these were men of good will. But I discovered that their oppression *wasn't* imposed out of ignorance. They didn't preach hurtful doctrine because they didn't know any better. They *knew* the truth and taught misinformation *on purpose.* They also knew their followers would spread the disinformation they taught, that harm would result. And they were OK with that.

The possibility had never occurred to me.

Suppressing accurate information is a crime against humanity, whether it's legal or not.

Mormon leaders also kept the documented history of Joseph Smith's polygamy from its members until just a few years ago. Even now, they insist that most of the polygamous marriages were non-sexual. I was taught at church that Mormons were kicked out of Missouri in the 1830s because Missouri was a slaveholding state and Mormons were against slavery. Church leaders kept hidden inconvenient details about the denomination's slave-owning members. An African American slave was even paid to the Church once as part of a member's tithe.

We all know some things. We also know there are things we don't know. The biggest problem, however, is in *not* knowing there are things we don't know because we've never heard of them.

Who knew to expect a sonic boom before we were able to fly fast enough to create one?

Does it matter that Bertolucci's lavish production of *The Last Emperor* leaves out the tiny detail that the last emperor of China was gay? Does it matter that not a single actor in the original *Star Wars* movie was black, not even among the extras? Does it matter when films on historic subjects erase the participation of blacks, Asians, or other non-whites from the story? How many of us are aware that six Chinese passengers were among the few survivors of the Titanic, and that the moment they reached the safe shores of America, they were immediately deported because the Chinese Exclusion Act would still be in force for another three decades?

Both distortion and omission of information cause widespread damage by shaping our cultural attitudes which then affect policy and law.

I was never taught that Christopher Columbus cut off the hands of native slaves and created a culture of such cruelty that before long, *half a million* Arawaks were dead. The denial of information about these human rights abuses is a separate human rights abuse itself, not only against African Americans and Native Americans but against everyone else as well, shaping our worldview and mindset so that many of us perpetuate systemic racism without even being aware of it.

U.S. mistreatment of the Japanese and other Asians is glossed over if taught at all. U.S. involvement in the assassination of leaders or in support of military coups—in the Democratic Republic of the Congo in 1961, in Chile in 1973, in Iran in 1953, and elsewhere—impact the lives of millions, affect international relations, affect virtually every person on the planet. We are able to simultaneously hate politicians, see faults with every elected leader we despise, and *also* believe "America" has never committed a single mistake in international policy. When we are kept ignorant of even the most basic knowledge of these interventions, we are unable to comprehend what is happening around the world today. Our ignorance has non-trivial consequences both here and abroad.

The misinformation and misdirection we receive every day affects what we eat, how we shop, the way we bury our dead. We grow up believing the way we fund and operate our police departments is how it's always been done, the way it *has* to be, while neither is true.

Lack of information keeps us blind to other possibilities. *That's one of its main functions.*

Tens of millions of Americans suffer from little or no health insurance. Our political leaders and our corporate media make deliberate choices to keep us ignorant of the various universal healthcare programs in every other developed country. Both Republicans and Democrats are told that single-payer or other universal healthcare programs are unrealistic and impractical. Every person in this country suffers, since even those of us with good healthcare are heavily impacted by those without.

The same goes for tuition-free college and vocational training. People are kept ignorant even of the information they *could* learn. Poverty, crime, cultural literacy, and everything else in our society is shaped by this suppression. *Millions* of people suffer entire lifetimes as a result. What kind of impact do thirty or forty million adults without degrees or vocational training have on the rest of the country, on our place in a global economy?

We call out female genital mutilation as a human rights abuse—and it's an appalling one—but we need to understand that a denial of post-secondary education is an abuse that also carries devastating consequences for women.

We are told that only having two major political parties is the norm, that anything else is for fringe radicals. That's not the way many functioning democracies around the world operate. It's impossible to keep Americans completely ignorant of what goes on in other countries, of course, but we can be and are taught that having other parties would never be viable here. We limit the scope (and amount) of our international news coverage. Keeping American voters ignorant of other possibilities denies us many of our basic human rights.

Why work for guaranteed childcare or a universal basic income if you've only heard a vague mention of them once or twice in your life? Why work to include dental and vision care with healthcare if you've always been taught separating them was simply the way things were done? When I lived in Italy, I was shocked to discover that one could attend an academic high school or a technical high school or a vocational high school. Each type even had sub-categories, and high school lasted five years, students typically graduating at 19. Who knew that we could adapt secondary education to meet the needs of the students, that accepting the one-size-fits-all status quo was a choice? It doesn't *feel* like a choice if we aren't aware there are options. But it is.

It's just that the choice is made by those controlling the information.

Not *everything* our political and religious leaders do is wrong, not *everything* reported by the media or taught in class is a lie crafted to deceive us. It's that we aren't given the information we need to know the difference and act accordingly.

That's by design. And this suppression of information, the deliberate spread of misinformation, and outright lying leave us without the time, energy, or funds to take care of ourselves, much less help anyone else. That, of course, allows those at the top to keep power and resources for themselves. It's one of the main motives for opposition to Net Neutrality.

When I left for the Missionary Training Center as a happy, dedicated nineteen-year-old, I soon discovered that I'd been lied to. I struggled almost every day for the next two years, virtually all of the suffering related to the lies and accompanying sense of betrayal I felt, not the experience itself. "Why didn't they tell me the truth?" I kept asking. "I would still have come. I just would have been better prepared."

We never know the full truth about anything, even in the sciences. We learn and modify and progress. That's not the same thing as denying the information we *do* know.

It will always be an uphill battle to teach the truth in schools or religious institutions, to elect leaders who have the interests of their voters at heart, to demand that journalists report the facts people need to know rather than the spin corporate executives want people to hear. We must do what we can to bring transparency and accuracy to each of those arenas, but in the meantime, we must learn to think critically, ask the right questions, verify what we can, and actively seek out the information we need.

In *The Kingdom of God is Within You*, Leo Tolstoy wrote, "The most difficult subjects can be explained to the most slow-witted man if he has not formed any idea of them already; but the simplest thing cannot be made clear to the most intelligent man if he is firmly persuaded that he knows already, without a shadow of a doubt, what is laid before him."

The one truth that is glaringly obvious? Knowledge is power and its possession creates an automatic conflict of interest. To share knowledge is to share power. And power is rarely granted freely. We must demand and take that knowledge, whether it's granted freely or not. Or we will find ourselves trapped, not in a hospital bed attached to a burning IV, but in an economic and intellectual prison, with no way out, suffering every day until we die.

Prerequisites for a Livable Society

"It's not fair to forgive student debt when I've paid mine off!" I hear conservatives say. "What makes *those people* so special? They should suffer, too!"

I understand the sentiment. That's exactly what I said when leukemia charities asked for donations after my mother died of leukemia at the age of forty-three. "How dare you try to make life better for others!" I screamed into the phone. "My mom is *dead*! If you couldn't save my mother, *no one* else should *ever* be saved! It's not *fair*!"

You know I didn't actually say anything so ridiculous, of course.

I will risk invoking Godwin's law, though, by pointing out that Republicans and moderate Democrats have become Soup Nazis. "No healthcare for you! No college for you! No Green New Deal for you!" Unless you count being left to fend for ourselves.

When I was promoted to senior companion during my Mormon mission to Italy, I was soon assigned a "greenie" straight from America, later becoming senior to a second new missionary. I helped them with irregular verbs. I explained any customs they needed to know. One of my first seniors had abandoned me during door approaches when I still couldn't understand anything Italians were saying to me. I found the practice cruel and tried instead to make life reasonably decent for my companions.

It honestly never occurred to me to be a jerk just because someone else had been a jerk to me.

When I worked at a credit union, we were held accountable to meet a certain weekly quota for home loan referrals. Yet we were forbidden from making any signage to spark interest. Because I talked with customers every day, I had a pretty good idea what signs would be effective and relayed the information to the marketing department.

No, *they* were trained and *they'd* be the ones to determine signage. If I overstepped my place, they'd report me to Human Resources.

So tellers throughout the credit union continued to fall short in their referrals.

I went to three other financial institutions and documented their signage, which was almost word-for-word what I'd suggested. After I submitted the information to the marketing department, they came out with new signs.

Yes, we *can* accept the status quo, even when it's terrible. We *can* make others as miserable as we were. We *can* refuse to make life better for the next generation.

That's what parents always say, isn't it? "I'm working three jobs because I want my kids to have a better life than I had."

Oh, wait.

Conservatives would have us believe that tuition-free college and vocational training lead to an entire population devoid of any responsibility.

Are we honestly saying that no Germans behave responsibly? No Danes? No Swedes? No Norwegians? No Finns? No French? No Argentinians? No Uruguayans? No Egyptians? No Turks?

My religiously conservative parents managed to live responsibly despite twelve years of "free" public education. Does irresponsibility only kick in after a thirteenth or fourteenth year?

In my mid-twenties, I started paying a monthly premium for life insurance. It was quite cheap, something like $7 a month. After paying for a few years, though, I began to worry. What if I was in a terrible accident just a week before the next monthly payment was due? What if I was too badly injured, maybe even comatose, to mail in a check? What if after three or four more weeks in the hospital, I died? My policy would have lapsed just when my beneficiaries finally needed it.

My parents had started a health insurance policy a few months before my mom became ill, but even so, the company decided she'd already been ill before the first premium and therefore decided not to cover any of her treatment. A week after she died, an employee from the billing department at the hospital called, demanding immediate and full payment. When Dad said he didn't have that much cash lying around, the agent said, "You could sell your home, couldn't you?"

So, I thought, perhaps I should build in a buffer for my life insurance. I began paying my premium one month ahead.

In response, the life insurance company began sending me notices not to pay the following month, but of course I did. The whole point of paying ahead was to stay ahead.

Irresponsible, I know.

Then the life insurance company sent me a refund check. I *couldn't* pay ahead. It wasn't allowed. The responsible thing to do, apparently, was to live one check away from losing everything.

It became clear the policy was built not to stay in effect. So I canceled it altogether.

When we force people into bankruptcy over medical bills, we're behaving irresponsibly. Likewise when we refuse to pay a living wage to full-time workers. We're also irresponsible when we refuse to provide college or vocational training to our citizens. We're expecting them to magically achieve a quota of success while denying them the tools to reach it. We're abandoning them at the door just to watch them squirm because we get some kind of perverse satisfaction from the hazing.

I give to leukemia research. I give to myelin research, too. I give to St. Jude Hospital and Doctors without Borders and the Himalayan Cataract Project because I don't think that making poor people suffer unnecessarily is responsible behavior. I give to organizations trying to clean up pollution. I give to the American Indian College Fund and PFLAG Scholarship Program.

But arbitrary donations here and there are not a responsible way to run a country. If we want to leave the spiritual welfare of our people up to volunteers, that's fine. But addressing the physical needs of our citizens can't responsibly be left up to the capricious leftovers of our free time and entertainment budgets.

"It's irresponsible to want free stuff! Only bums want to take, take, take!"

You mean like demanding federal taxes from the residents of Washington DC without allowing them representation? Or did you mean disbanding the elected officials of Flint, Michigan to take their money and then poison the town's inhabitants with lead-tainted water? Perhaps you meant taking people off the street and holding them in detention for years without even charging them, much less trying them in court?

There's plenty of taking to go around, plenty of irresponsibility, plenty of suffering and paying one's dues. So let's just concentrate on the main point:

It doesn't matter if healthcare and education and clean water and a living wage are "rights." If we want to live in a community not plagued with homelessness and crime and unrest, if we want to live in a country capable of competing successfully on a global level, we must treat our citizens as resources to be cultivated, not pests to be squashed.

We must stop thinking about these programs and policies as "entitlements." They're simply prerequisites for a livable society and a habitable planet.

Let's start behaving more responsibly and take care of our human resources.

Successful Citizens Are the Key to a Successful Nation

Many Americans worry that the U.S. is losing ground to China, Russia, or other rising global powers. We think drilling for more oil or banning immigrants or enacting harsher prison sentences will get us back on top or, at the very least, keep us from slipping further off the winner's podium.

However, those aren't the most effective strategies for making America #1. We can't succeed without making the success of everyday Americans not only "possible" but routine. Here are seven difficult ways for the U.S. to win, and one easy way to lose:

First, we must **reduce income inequality**. A living wage is not a giveaway. By definition, folks are working for it. We must raise the minimum wage so that no one working 40 hours a week lives below the poverty level. We also need a comparable minimum Social Security payment. And there's a great deal of evidence that Universal Basic Income is effective.

Affordable housing must actually be affordable if we are to decrease our growing homeless population.

Many of our most successful corporations are already headquartered elsewhere or have sent a majority of their jobs overseas. When we can only ensure success for the top 1% of our population, we have no leverage to keep corporations or their jobs—and the funds to pay them—here.

We need **universal healthcare**. Every other industrialized nation in the world, and even a few developing countries, guarantee healthcare to all their citizens. If we want to attract and keep the best minds and talents, healthcare must be part of the incentive package. Dental, vision, and mental healthcare must be included as well. We can't keep a competitive economy when over half a million Americans are forced to declare bankruptcy every year over medical debt.

When the number of Americans affected by crushing medical debt is added to the number of full-time workers living below the poverty level on subsistence wages, we already have a population so heavily burdened we can only continue to slip further away from a leading position in the global economy.

The U.S. must ensure **tuition-free college and vocational training**. Like universal healthcare, free or nearly free postsecondary education is guaranteed by many other countries. Some of the best international students will go elsewhere for their education and then work in those other countries as well. We're creating our own competitors. And we can't even concentrate on developing our homegrown students because millions here simply can't afford our skyrocketing tuition.

Even those who take out student loans are then burdened for twenty or thirty years with debt that prevents them from buying a home, making other consumer purchases, having more children, or making financial investments in their own future. And their future is America's future.

Just as a sports team can't be successful unless its players are given the training and other resources they need, a country that refuses to ensure that its citizens are skilled and educated cannot hope to remain a world leader.

Universal pre-k and subsidized childcare are non-negotiable if we want successful adults. Workers don't mysteriously materialize out of nowhere at the age of eighteen, prepared to make America's economy competitive. We must begin by valuing childcare and childhood education. And in a digital economy, for kids to succeed in school, they need free access to high-speed internet.

Is such access a "right"? It doesn't really matter. Full access to high-speed internet is *necessary* if we hope to have a skilled population that can compete on the world stage.

Strong, capable adults come from nurtured, educated children.

Fare-free public transportation allows even the poorest folks to get to work and back. It's also essential if we want to address the climate crisis. Those with no transportation or access to childcare may be good stay-at-home parents, but they're certainly not contributing to a successful global economy. They often, however, are forced to depend on public assistance. It doesn't matter if poverty and dependence are technically our goals if they're still the consistent outcome. If we want workers to get to work, we must make achieving that something less than a daily Herculean effort.

We must **decriminalize addiction, provide subsidized rehab, and eliminate private prisons**. The war on drugs has led the U.S. to inflict enormous casualties on its own citizens. Legalizing some recreational drugs and decriminalizing others will save our country hundreds of millions of dollars a year, plus create taxable income. It also allows us to stop deliberately destroying the lives of millions of our citizens, a plus even if it didn't save money, which it does. Our current system of creating millions of unemployable workers each year with felony convictions ensures increasing poverty—or criminal enterprise as the only viable way to earn money. Destroying our own populace isn't an effective way to compete globally.

The last and arguably most important way to maintain or raise our position is to **tackle the climate crisis head-on**. We must become a global leader in products and services for greener forms of energy. We need to find the most effective, least destructive ways to incorporate wind, solar, thermal, or other methods of extracting and storing energy.

Burying our head in the tar sands won't change reality. *Whichever* country develops the best technology and infrastructure to move us away from fossil fuels, to remove carbon from the atmosphere, and to deal with the no longer preventable changes that are now too late to avoid, *will* be the leader of the world. If that's not us, it will be China or

Russia or India or someone else. It won't be—*can't* be—the U.S.

We'll *have* to do it eventually, of course, whether we want to or not, whether we come in last or not, so we may as well make a goal to be the best at it.

There are all sorts of other things we could implement—require all high school graduates to master two foreign languages, require a semester abroad for every college degree, or a year of teaching ESL to immigrants. We could require community service instead of military service and retrofit buildings with energy-efficient windows or solar panels or whatever, teaching marketable skills in the process. There are many other things we could do to improve our country, but we only NEED these seven.

And we'll pay for these things one way or another. Prisons aren't cheap. Neither are riots in response to racism and other forms of oppression. Cleaning up oil spills or water polluted by fracking isn't free. Neither is the destruction caused by longer wildfire and stronger hurricane seasons. Droughts and floods aren't cheap. Neither is relocating coastal communities.

We can divert hundreds of billions from our military budget and still fund at a level four times that of either China or Russia. We can tax corporations and the wealthy at the same levels we did in the 1950s and have more than enough funds to implement these changes.

So what's the **one easy, sure way for America to fail**? Choosing austerity programs. This, of course, can be broken down into smaller pieces—pitting workers against each other, taxing everyone except the rich, cutting back on every form of assistance, trickle-down economics—but it's all basically the same thing. When we structure every benefit to favor the top 1% of citizens and weigh down the other 99%, we ensure with absolute certainty that 99% of our population will not be able to compete effectively with the Chinese or Russians.

Just as it's easier to deface property than to construct it, just as it's easier to burn a book than to write one, it's easier to choose austerity over the difficult programs we'll need to lift our country.

It boils down to this: do we *want* healthy, educated, well-balanced adults? Then we'd better not start two decades after their most formative years. Do we want a skilled, educated, debt-free population capable of competing globally in every major industry? Then we'd better stop throwing up as many barriers as possible. We must accept responsibility for the workforce we do—or don't—create.

None of these winning strategies is easy. But then, no one wins a gold medal by putting off strenuous workouts. No one is named valedictorian for shrugging off chemistry and literature classes. No one wins a Nobel Peace Prize for justifying mass incarceration and extrajudicial killings.

There's only one way to be competitive on the world stage, and that's by making our citizens successful. We don't *have* to do it, of course. We *can* let the inertia of our current poor policies keep dragging us down.

That's certainly the easier path.

But if we want to succeed, we'll need to stop deifying oppression in all its forms. We must change our downward course by telling officials already in office exactly what we demand, and only support those candidates in future elections who are willing to take immediate action.

Sound hard?

Well, you didn't think it would be easy, did you?

So let's get to work.

Section 4: Withstanding Criticism and Disappointment

Make the Apocalypse Great Again

I never thought of *Who Framed Roger Rabbit?* as a documentary. A world where real people interacted with living cartoon characters was preposterous. But as I watched the former president's lawyer melting on camera during the last days of the administration, I realized the movie was downright prophetic—scripture for the surreal times we live in.

At the Baptist high school I attended, we watched a film about the Tribulation. Three young women find themselves left behind after the Rapture and decide, a bit late, to become Christians. They're persecuted, betrayed, and in the end face execution. The final scene reveals a guillotine, with the main character screaming in terror when she realizes her fate.

As a Mormon, I'd also been raised with an apocalyptic worldview. Latter-day Saints didn't believe in the Rapture, but we did believe in years of suffering before Armageddon ushered in the Second Coming. Following the Prophet's orders, my parents stored a Year's Supply of food and other provisions. My dad bought guns so we could defend our stash from hungry neighbors. My Patriarchal Blessing promised me strength and wisdom to lead others through the perilous times ahead.

Anticipating the inevitable horrors was as normal as looking forward to high school graduation, two years as a full-time missionary, a college education, temple marriage, and raising children of my own. Dread was simply part of life.

And now, as I watch right-wing Christians mount an insurrection, as I hear them threaten to kidnap or hang or otherwise execute Satan-worshipping cannibals, as I hear their claims that space lasers ignited wildfires in California, that an artificial, mechanized Biden ordered fake snow to blanket Texas, as I watch them worship a golden statue of their pagan messiah, I'm… baffled.

I *thought* I would feel terror in the face of impending doom. And I suppose I do. But what I feel most is befuddlement.

This is the buffoon people have chosen to follow to their damnation? *These* are the doctrines they believe? That alien lizard people, in cahoot with Jews, control D.C. and the media? That folks who want to stop the slaughter of Black people are their arch enemies? That tearing brown children away from their parents—not incidentally, but as a political strategy—is God's will?

We all watched while maskless "patriots" smirked with glee, refusing to protect other elected officials from a deadly virus, as they hid from a rampaging mob.

These "Christians" laughed. Giggled.

I'd watched the first three seasons of *Handmaid's Tale* with growing anxiety, understanding how close we were to such a dystopian world.

I didn't expect we'd instead be living the *Life of Brian*.

How did we get demagogues channeling Elmer Fudd?

Why is our intrigue that of Boris and Natasha?

Throughout my youth, I feared that those following the Beast would be brutish, terrifying, cruel, and vindictive. And they certainly are.

What I didn't expect was that they'd *also* be pathetic and absurd.

As we debate replacing our racist national anthem, perhaps we should consider Ella Fitzgerald's, "Bewitched, Bothered, and Bewildered," surely a song more befitting our current *Twilight Zone* political environment.

Almost half the country has willingly, on purpose, chosen hero worship over policy.

I lived a stone's throw from Pompeii when I worked as a missionary in Naples. I studied the Fall of the Roman Empire after I resumed my college classes back in the U.S. The long, complex history of that region seemed deeply sad, painfully tragic.

I had no idea that witnessing the Fall of the American Empire, with millions of people choosing, on purpose, to create the tribulations of the Last Days of their own free will, would be so… embarrassing.

I'd grown up anticipating the End of Times as something akin to a worldwide Nazi concentration camp. I'd read up on Holocaust literature to prepare myself for what lay ahead.

Instead, we got the Marshmallow Man from *Ghostbusters.* The Penguin from *Batman.* Vizzini from *The Princess Bride.*

We follow the news in a daze, feeling both perplexed and ashamed. We're Mary Tyler Moore, torn between laughing and crying during the funeral of Chuckles the Clown.

But we must stop feeling shocked, stop asking ourselves if this is all really happening.

It is.

If we want America to remain a free democracy, or even a free republic, we'd better start addressing the basic needs we all have—for healthcare, a living wage, and college education or vocational training for all.

Because the enemy isn't the false messiah or those who worship him. The enemy is ignoring the gaping needs that created them.

Troll Others and Be the Worse for It

I don't use social media much, even though authors trying to build a following are "supposed" to. There's a climate crisis on social media almost as dangerous as the one we see wreaking havoc across the globe through melting glaciers, stronger hurricanes, and longer fire seasons. Aside from slogging through deliberate disinformation, we too often end up in arguments with actual friends. You know, the kind we've known in real life for years, not folks we've met in cyberspace.

Studies suggest that people who spend too much time on social media, especially those who start their day with it, often feel more depressed or anxious or irritable. We've all heard the term "doomscrolling."

So I spend less and less of my time online. But I do check in briefly a couple of times a day because I have friends I'm not able to keep up with any other way. Thankfully, I know a few folks who go out of their way to post mostly positive or useful information.

Recently, I read a post lamenting Biden's refusal to forgive student loan debt. Not all of the debt, of course, or $50K of it, not even $10K. He's "considering." He's "studying the issue." He wants to make sure that if he does it, he does it "right."

I typed a quick comment. "And so we wait and wait and wait and wait and…"

Then I moved on with my day, hopping onto my stationary bicycle to get in a little exercise while watching another episode of *The Art of Crime*, a fun show about mismatched detectives solving murders in Paris related to famous works of art.

Hours later, I checked back in on social media to do my second and final tour of the day.

And saw a response to my earlier comment. “Keep waiting. No one owes you anything.”

I hate to admit I was shocked.

You’d think by this point I’d be well aware of the vitriol out there. And this was relatively tame compared to other comments I’ve received. But my own comment hadn’t indicated I wanted *my* student loan forgiven. I’ve been paying down on it for over twenty years. While I would be happy to have the last of it forgiven, my remaining debt is manageable. I was thinking about the millions of others still paying on $60K or $80K or $110K loans.

And I was also pointing out that all this “deliberation” was no more than a show. Any national leader who can’t make up their mind on an issue that’s been in the headlines for years is either not paying attention (hardly something to boast about) or stringing us along (not such a great thing to boast about, either).

But this troll went out of her way to be mean.

When I first came out and started going to gay bars, other men would warn me about this bar or that one. "Lots of trolls over there."

Trolls, I learned, were old, lecherous gay men no one wanted to be with. They'd grope you without permission. Some of the nicer older men I met in those early years would make an effort not to be too aggressive. "I don't want to be a troll," they'd tell me.

I hoped I'd never become one myself.

These days, it looks like thousands and thousands of folks, men and women of all ages, mostly straight but sometimes gay, happily choose to be the most disgusting trolls possible, trolls far more repulsive than any of the old, lecherous men I ever met.

Online trolls aspire to be the Fred Phelps of cyberspace. Their guiding motto isn't "What would Jesus do?" but "What would Joe McCarthy do?" They want to cultivate hatred and anger like crops, boasting of their wins as if they'd presented the prize pumpkin at a county fair.

Compassion is their Kryptonite and they do whatever they can to destroy it.

We've all dealt with these folks. They're inescapable, and giddily so. One of their key rhetorical strategies is to misframe the question. My support for forgiving student loan debt isn't because I think the government or any other American "owes" it to us.

But leaders can recognize the many ways having an educated population not saddled with debt is good not only for them but for everyone else as well. If anything, we owe it to ourselves.

When I first began facing my affectional orientation, I started attending a "Coming Out" support group. One evening, I said something about feeling mystified that gay men, who understood firsthand how awful discrimination was, could in turn discriminate against women or Black people or anyone else.

"Ah," one of the moderators said, "that's because you have internalized homophobia."

"Huh?"

"You still think that as a gay person you have to be better than straight people. It's like a woman wanting better grades to show she's as smart as her male classmates. It's like a Black person speaking better than white coworkers to show he's as competent. But gay people are entitled to be just as imperfect as anyone else."

Decades later, I still disagree with that concept. Of course, the moderator was right that we don't need to prove ourselves to anyone. The reason we develop empathy is to make society better, and we can only develop that empathy by putting ourselves in someone else's situation. While I may never understand more than a fraction of what it is to face other forms of bias, I know *enough* to be able to extrapolate and act accordingly. I know enough to be open to learning more.

No one, not even the most privileged among us, can reach adulthood without having experienced *some* form of oppression or cruelty or injustice. If we fail to use those experiences to learn how to treat each other more humanely, that's a choice we've made. And it's nothing to boast about.

Do we *owe* anyone kindness or justice? Do we *owe* anyone healthcare or education or a habitable planet?

If we're trolls, the answer is quite clearly no.

I hope, though, we can aspire to something a little greater. That enough of us will finally understand the best way to lift ourselves is to lift everyone around us, too.

To Be an Ally or Not to Be

White activists should confront the epidemic of police killings of unarmed blacks. Straight folks should fight for LGBTQ rights. Christians should protest discrimination against Muslims. Men should demand passage of the Equal Rights Amendment.

Some oppressed or marginalized groups actively seek allies, but others see them as infiltrators complicit in their oppression. Rebuffing allies, though, is playing into the hands of those who keep their power by manipulating women and gays and blacks and Latinos and Native Americans to attack each other. Divide and conquer has been a successful strategy for centuries. We must resist the temptation to turn away allies and instead work to develop solidarity.

Shortly after I came out, I attended a Single Adult activity at church. One of the young women made a comment about a gay character on TV, a remarkable event back in the mid-1980s. "Can you believe how perverted the world is getting?" she asked.

I watched how my best friend, the only person in the room who knew my secret, reacted. He said nothing. Afterward, I asked him why.

He immediately grew angry. "People always want me to stick up for them! This is your fight, not mine!"

I suppose he was right, but I remember thinking, "How does an oppressed group ever gain any power if no one in the majority ever joins their fight?" Even as a closeted, self-loathing, celibate gay man, terrified of being found out, I stood up for gays. I could have done it during the Single Adult activity, but I wanted to see what my friend would do.

Or wouldn't do.

Some of my older white friends were Freedom Riders in the Deep South. They put their lives on the line. They don't want credit for it. They would just prefer to be allowed to contribute to the cause of justice and equality without being vilified as "trying to make this about them."

I understand rage. Being excommunicated from the Mormon Church for insisting on my right to seek love and companionship of my choosing left me bitter for years. Growing up in the south, where even "nice" people used the N-word, I was surprised the Rodney King riots in Los Angeles didn't spread across the entire country. Even with abundant exposure to black points of view, with years of interaction with blacks at all levels of society, I constantly discovered more layers of implicit bias I never realized I had.

Blacks certainly need to call us out when we do or say stupid or harmful things. To be clear, of course, it's not anyone else's job to teach us everything. There are tons of material we can access to teach ourselves. But we can't master all the information overnight, and we can't delay joining the fight for equality until we've perfected our knowledge and character.

Recently, a friend on Facebook posted a link to a new song by Taylor Swift called "You Need to Calm Down," where she stands up for gay rights. Some responded with an article from *The Onion.* "Taylor Swift Inspires Teen to Come Out as Straight Woman Needing to Be at Center of Gay Rights Narrative." Then someone complained about Taylor Swift's father who was such "a monster" that the Indigo Girls wrote a song about him.

I don't think Taylor Swift is responsible for her father's behavior. I also don't think that because Taylor is a white, rich heterosexual that we should label her work as an ally self-serving. If her song serves us, I'm fine with it serving her as well.

I don't need perfect allies.

There are no perfect allies.

I'm not sure how effective Taylor Swift or anyone else would be if they had to take a vow of poverty or undergo conversion therapy before joining the fight.

We can correct or chastise or guide or debate, but it is self-defeating to toss allies into a moral waste bin.

In fourth grade, I saw a friend of mine being picked on during recess. A complete wimp then as now, I summoned up what little courage I had and walked up to the bullies. "Leave him alone," I said, using all the wit and wisdom at my disposal.

The bullies walked away, and my friend turned to me in anger. "I don't need your help!" he shouted before storming off.

I expect my friend was more embarrassed than angry, but even if I may have felt slightly hurt, my overwhelming reaction at the time was bewilderment. In his situation, I'd have welcomed any help I could get. And I *had* been in his situation many times.

I saw *To Kill a Mockingbird* for the first time as an adult and immediately loved it. Many years would pass before I'd recognize the "white savior" issue. But I do wonder how else that story could have been told. Should a black lawyer have come to town? Should the black townspeople have rioted and burned the courthouse down? All viable options, I suppose. Stories can be told in many ways, and clearly more stories must be told from multiple black perspectives.

But white people have a stake in equality, too, and the character of Atticus Finch had every right to make what little contribution he could.

And really, the story isn't even about racism. That's just a vehicle for the real point, standing up to do the right thing even when most of your friends and peers are against you, even when you do it at great personal and professional risk. The point could have been made using homophobia instead of racism as the background. It could have been women's rights or anti-Semitism or pollution or anything else. It was the standing up that mattered, though using a black character as a vehicle for the white character to defy unjust societal norms is problematic as well. There's also the problem with Atticus dismissing the woman who claims to have been raped. I'm not sure Harper Lee used the best scenarios to make her point.

But I'm also not sure books and movies and authors have to be perfect to be useful.

The English movie *Pride* tells the true story of gay activists in the 1980's who rallied behind striking coal miners. Some gays refused to help, saying that the strikers were exactly the kind of guys who'd beaten them up as kids. Then lesbians broke from the group because they didn't want to be lumped with the men. And many of the strikers didn't want to be associated with either faggots *or* dykes.

After a homophobic union leader forces the gay activists out, other union supporters discover that the gay group has raised more money to support them than any other group.

Thirty years later, coal miners were among the strongest supporters when gay rights finally came up for a vote in the country.

"Androcles and the Lion" is effective as a fable because it tells a universal truth.

History has proven time and again that solidarity makes us stronger than we can ever be when we allow oppressors to divide us and waste our time and energy fighting each other instead of directing our energies against them.

No one wants to be undermined by an ally's misguided approach. Gay people don't want heterosexuals calling all the shots in their organizations. Women don't need men telling them the "right" way to protest. Blacks don't need whites ordering them about.

But debates over strategy and policy are essential. Allies need to be able to participate in those discussions, even if they aren't—and shouldn't be—in charge. Solidarity is always a work in progress, but the rewards are worth the effort.

I am a white gay male, an ex-Mormon atheist. Women's equality is essential for me if I'm to have a good life. Racial equality is essential for me to have a good life. Workers' rights are essential for me to have a good life.

Martin Luther King, Jr. stated it clearly. "Injustice anywhere is a threat to justice everywhere."

I have a moral obligation to help oppressed groups to which I don't belong.

I also have self-interest.

Members of every oppressed group need to fight for their rights. Members of every other oppressed group, and every decent human being belonging to every privileged group, must join together in solidarity to fight for the rights of all who don't have them now. Equality and justice aren't scarce resources. The more we give to more people, the more there is for everyone.

We can't abdicate our responsibility out of fear we'll be reprimanded and embarrassed. Let's be the best allies we can be, and let's accept the imperfect help offered to us in our own battles anywhere we can find it.

Virtue Signaling, Mansplaining, and Whitesplaining

How often do you scroll through social media and find a post that begins, "This is just a test to see who is a real friend, who will read this post to the end and then copy and paste—not Like or share—and write 'done' in the comments…"

I always stop right there. Whether or not I'm a "real friend," I know this person isn't if he or she feels compelled to test me all the time.

A woman I know likes to discuss important theological, political, and moral points with others. If a man joins in and says anything that isn't 100% in agreement, he's immediately called out for mansplaining. His only options are to say nothing, be a yes man, or be a misogynist. In this woman's mind, he cannot ever offer anything useful of his own.

To be fair, many men *are* guilty of every aspect of mansplaining—arrogance, condescension, insensitivity, ignorance, and everything else that goes along with the term. The same is true when white people try to take part in discussions of race, bias, and privilege. And I see people of almost every race, gender, sexual orientation, and physical ability send out virtue signals, trying to shame others who aren't as woke as they are.

As a white, cisgender male, albeit gay, I'm constantly aware that my experience makes almost anything I say on issues of bias and discrimination suspect. I'm far more likely than most to have biases I'm still unaware of even after decades of observation and attempts at self-awareness and improvement.

As a writer, I learned early on that any hope I had of producing a good story or essay depended largely on how much outside input I could gather on my work. The more friends and writers who critiqued my work, the better my revision would be. And if I could enlist others to critique the next version of the piece as well, the following revision would be even stronger.

Just because I benefit from critiques doesn't mean I don't have something useful to contribute of my own, something worth critiquing in the first place.

Listening, though, really hearing not only what people say but why they say it, is the only way to benefit from those critiques. So often in college workshops, when students would hear what other classmates or the instructor had to say, the student being critiqued would respond, "Well, you just don't understand what I'm going for here. You read it too fast. You didn't give it enough thought." On and on, they'd defend their original version of the work, their ego so deeply invested in "being a good writer" that they were afraid to admit they weren't already brilliant.

All throughout high school and college, I heard, "You have such potential as a writer." But I didn't want "potential." I wanted to *be* a good writer.

In the current atmosphere of virtue signaling, many of us are so afraid to be labeled racist or sexist or homophobic or xenophobic that we insist on defending our position rather than admit that it might need a little revising. When we talk to a black colleague, we try to "subtly" insert a list of all the good things we've done to combat racism. We mention how we learned so much living in a mixed neighborhood. We want to be absolved of the crimes of our ancestors. We want to be absolved of our own past actions. We want to be absolved of our ongoing complicit support of the powerful structural racism everywhere in our culture.

An abuse victim doesn't owe their abuser a pat on the back for being so magnanimous as to stop abusing them or, more accurately, abusing them a little less.

I've been writing for fifty years. I've been publishing for almost thirty. I took writing workshops as an undergraduate and again in grad school before going on to earn a second Master's degree in writing. I'm a professional proofreader, a volunteer slush pile reader, a judge in writing contests. I've published hundreds of stories and essays, over 50 books. And I'm under no delusion that "I've arrived." I will *always* need others to point out where I need to tighten the wording, delete an unproductive concept, add a vital point I'd somehow completely omitted.

The correct response in these situations is, "Thank you for taking the time to point out what I did wrong."

My mother dreamed of being a writer. When my parents first married, they saved every penny, never splurging on so much as a Coke. But my mom asked my dad to pay for a correspondence course so she could become a writer. And after successfully finishing her first story, she sent it off to a magazine. The editor was even kind enough to offer a brief critique along with his rejection.

My mother never wrote another story.

Whatever that loss meant to her, I can't know. I only discovered all this when going through her papers after she died. But the loss to me is enormous. I grieve that she had no one in her life to encourage her to learn and grow and become that writer she surely had the potential of being. The blow to her ego when she discovered she wasn't competent right from the start crushed her spirit and was so shameful it was easier to give up her goals altogether than forge her way ahead.

And yet even my reflections here subtly convey the message that *I* was stronger than she was. *I* was better.

"You read three books on anti-racism? Well, *I* read five."

"You cried when terrorists bombed people in Paris? Well, *I* cried when people were bombed in Syria."

"You donated to ten environmental groups? Well, *I* was part of a blockade to stop an oil tanker."

OK. You're better than I am. I concede the point. But this bizarre morality contest does nothing to advance justice and equality. Most of us are far more likely to run from an experience that will lead to shame than embrace it, and those who care about these issues come to the battle already primed for humiliation. How many times have we let a secret go untold, a bad decision uncorrected, because we were too embarrassed to let our loved ones know about it?

It's almost impossible, unfortunately, for us to avoid judging others when we've put so much effort into our own writing or gym workouts or small business, much less our anti-racist, anti-sexist, and anti-homophobic work, which reflects our innermost core.

I used to believe there would be a point when I'd accomplished achieving the eradication of my personal biases and could then focus only on "helping society." It's disconcerting to realize I'm always going to do and say things that are racist and sexist. Not intentionally, I hope, but as my first writing instructor pointed out, "It doesn't matter what you meant. What the reader is seeing is X." Just as I'll always need critiques from others to help me sharpen my writing skills, I'll need to be called out by allies to help me succeed in anti-racism and anti-sexism. What I don't need, what no social justice movement needs, are those who invest so much of their energy telling everyone else how stupid and insensitive they are.

My first day in Organic Chemistry 1001, the professor stood in front of the room and said something along the lines of, "Most of you are pre-med. You think you're so smart. But I'm going to make sure at least half of you fail this class."

When I heard my professor smugly condemning his students, I dropped the class and signed up with another professor, one whose goal was to teach us, to help us succeed, not show how superior he was. Sure, as a student, it was ultimately my responsibility to learn the material, regardless of the goals or competency of the instructor. So I took responsibility for putting myself in an environment where I could learn the most.

I made A's in both Organic Chemistry 1001 and 1002. I also chose professors whose main goal was to teach, not belittle, for the other five chemistry courses I needed. I made A's in all of them.

Bully for me.

That hardly means I'm a chemistry pro. The classmate leading our study group went on to earn a PhD and become a chemistry professor, sharing photos online of her work with poison dart frogs in Central America. But even she is still always learning. And her goal is to engage students, not alienate them.

On Facebook recently, I read a post from the friend who accuses every man of mansplaining. She was lambasting progressives who "voted for Trump." For the past three years, she's made repeated claims about how this supposedly large number of her friends completely swayed the election against Clinton. As the protests against police brutality intensified and COVID continued to run amok across the nation, she said something along the lines of, "I guess this plan of progressives to elect Trump is working out pretty well for you, isn't it?"

I was tempted to respond, "Are you insane?" but that was exactly what she was looking for, some fool who would dare argue with her, an opportunity to lash out at her "friends." It was clear she would rather cause more division by "proving" she was right than actually do anything to bring people over to her position, a position she felt was essential if progress was to be made. But she would risk that progress just to have the opportunity to bait someone to disagree so she could eviscerate them. That way she could prove her superiority, which was far more important than anything else.

If no legitimate discussion can be had on a topic without "opponents" being labeled as racist, sexist, ignorant, stupid, and biased, then no progress can be made at all. That's bad enough if the people trying to communicate are on "opposite sides." But when we're supposedly on the same side, just in slightly different positions on that side, and all conversation is cut off, then being the most virtuous, the smartest, the most anti-racist, the most feminist, the best pro-LGBTQ person alive isn't much help to anyone, even to that most remarkable, incredible person.

As a writer, I had to read hundreds of books just to have a baseline of what competency looked like. I had to seek out writing workshops, ask for Independent Study courses to create extra workshops. I had to pursue a second Master's degree even though doing so wouldn't help further my career, only help me hone my craft. I accept that

I need to put in the same level of work to become a better human rights advocate.

It's not pleasant to learn I've said or done something insensitive or damaging. But if I have, denying it won't change the facts. I committed a long time ago not to stop writing like my mother did, just because an authority figure didn't approve of my contribution. I will never be the world's greatest writer. I will also never be the world's most understanding, most powerful, most effective advocate of racial and gender equality. I'll never come up with the best ideas to address the climate crisis. Even after I listen to valid criticism and improve, I'll still fall short.

Can there be *any* excuse that despite years of hearing vague mentions of Juneteenth, it wasn't until the year George Floyd was killed that I finally looked it up?

Diversity trainers often begin their training with the warning, "You're going to have to accept feeling uncomfortable." If I'm mortified when a proofreader points out that I spelled "harelip" as "hairlip," that I used the word "whom" incorrectly, that I neglected to do my research and included anachronisms in my historical fiction, I'm certainly going to feel self-loathing when I realize I've contributed yet again—now, today—to a cultural bias that crushes and kills others.

But my "feeling bad" about my actions hardly makes me the victim here. It's incredibly self-centered for white folks to make a discussion on race all about us, but in the end, I'm the only racist whose behavior I have any chance of modifying. So I'll channel the positive and the negative as best I can to do that.

Sometimes, I can develop a remarkably decent essay in two hours. Yet I've been working for several weeks on this one, knowing that within another few weeks or months, I'll look back and cringe over some stupid, ignorant thing I said. I'm not so blind I can't see that all my mansplaining and whitesplaining in these pages isn't a blatant attempt to deflect from my shortcomings. I'm giving myself an out, a pass, spending far more energy on proving I'm really and truly one of the good guys than on repairing damage.

I can accept that others are better at anti-racism than I am. But I must also acknowledge that "good" people are still perfectly capable of racist behavior. If we must, let's go ahead and believe that we're good.

So what? We need to stop making self-validation the goal. The goal is to dismantle racism.

Writing about it forces me to face disturbing realities rather than push them aside. I hope that reading my work helps others keep the problem in focus as well.

I've benefitted from my privilege for six decades. I'll never "arrive" at "redemption." Because there is no redemption. There is at best progress. Whatever "potential" I have, it's not a potential for perfect understanding and action.

But I won't be silent just because I make mistakes. Because I do believe that Silence = Death, that Silence =

Betrayal. And that the greatest mistake of all is to cede the obligation to solve problems to someone else… and the work required to make those solutions a reality.

Keeping the Pantry Full: Freedom and Justice Demand Constant Vigilance

"I can't wait till the Mueller report comes out."

"I can't wait until the mid-term elections in 2018."

"I can't wait till we elect a new president in 2020."

"We'll never achieve equality until we abandon capitalism and adopt socialism."

"I can't wait until the mid-term elections in 2022."

Almost everyone I know is working hard to get us out of the terrible political predicament we're currently in, but only a handful seem to recognize that none of these things is a permanent fix. Justice, freedom, and equality don't have fairy tale endings. There's no moment after which we can live happily ever after. Maintaining freedom and justice and equality will be a constant battle, not only in our lifetimes but forever.

Have we ever heard someone say, "I finally got all the weeds out of my yard. I never have to worry about that nasty task again"?

Have we heard anyone say, "Whew. I'm finally down to my ideal weight and BMI. Now I can stop exercising and watching what I eat"?

Or "I finally have the right to marry, and I've married the man of my dreams. It's all coasting from here"?

Whatever our personal end goals are for "progress," whether that be electing anyone other than Trump, or trying to get Democrats to move to the left, or to implement full-fledged socialism, Election Day is not the end of the struggle. The "Revolution" is not the end.

The work we do is hard. We want it to be over. We want to "win" and finally have a chance to breathe, but the painful truth is we can never relax.

Critics of reform point out that reforms can always be undone. That's true. But revolution and complete overhaul can be undone, too. The people's revolution in Russia didn't bring about lasting change. Within a decade, socialism had been corrupted into communism. Before long, Russia and then the Soviet Union were oppressive tyrannies. After "the revolution" in Cuba, its citizens still faced a dictatorship that threw LGBTQ folks and dissenters into prison.

Everything can be undone. That doesn't mean we shouldn't push Dems to the left, that we shouldn't try to shift to Democratic Socialism, that we shouldn't bring about Trotsky socialism. It just means that whatever path we choose, we must realize our end goals are no more secure than anyone else's. Your system may very well be better than my system, but it's every bit as susceptible to failure as any other.

That's because human beings will be implementing and sustaining each and every type of system we ever develop, and no humans of any persuasion are perfect. It seems a trite and obvious point, but every day I see people who think that if they get *their* way, if *their* idea of the perfect candidate or perfect policy or perfect economic or political system is victorious, we'll finally be OK.

We can be better, but we'll never be OK.

That doesn't mean we fall into cynicism or despair. We just need realistic expectations.

Protecting and preserving something great is a never-ending battle. Religious fanatics in the past decade have destroyed Persian artifacts dating back nearly 2000 years. Catholic invaders 500 years ago destroyed every Mayan book they could find. Thousands of temples, churches, synagogues, and mosques around the world, some of them hundreds of years old, have been destroyed over the years by enemies of the worshippers who met there.

We can preserve national parks against predators (you know, coal and oil companies, loggers, off-road recreational vehicles) every day for decades and decades, but all that work can be undone overnight once one of those predators finally gets in. It's far easier to cut down a 2000-year-old tree than it is to protect it every day against every possible threat.

Holocaust survivors are murdered 70 years after their liberation from the camps. We can clean up Superfund sites, and they can be polluted once again. We can develop antibiotics, and bacteria can evolve to withstand them.

Our work demanding justice and equality doesn't have an end date. There will *never* be a time when we can let our guard down.

This necessity for constant vigilance is true in every other part of our lives. Why in the world would we expect something different in the political and economic world? Because *those* things are simpler, smaller, and easier to control?

We must fight to make the world a better place, but we must do so with the understanding that such an endeavor requires a permanent commitment. Every advance we achieve must be supervised and monitored. We must always maintain oversight. We must continually keep pressure on all involved to preserve each and every victory.

Part of that is recruiting and training the next generation, and the one after that, to take over the fight when we're too old and tired to keep going. Another part is to let them come up with ideas and plans of their own. We can tag team with others so we can take a temporary break in the battle when we're weary.

Because while we're edified by helping, we can also be damaged by the emotional investment it requires.

It helps to remember that past leaders may have been tremendous heroes but that doesn't make every word they wrote scripture. If bacteria can adapt to new conditions, we can, too.

We just returned from the dentist with clean teeth and a clean bill of health, with no cavities or gum disease? That's great, but we'd better keep brushing and flossing. If a new prophylactic treatment becomes available, we'd be wise to include it.

Folks in AA take things “one day at a time.” They understand a universal truth, that one must always maintain constant vigilance, that even thirty or forty years of sobriety can be lost with a single night of drinking.

When my doctor told me I had to do three or more daily finger sticks to monitor my diabetes, I insisted on using a 14-day continuous glucose monitoring device instead. “It’s not as good,” he insisted. “You need instant results.”

“Doctor,” I replied, “you’re going to need to deal with the patient you have, not the one you wish you had.”

When I recounted the story to my husband, he said, “That’s the way we handle our marriage, isn’t it? We deal with the partner we have, not the one we wish we had.”

It sounds offensive, but the reality is that no patient is perfect, no spouse is perfect. If we refuse to treat patients until they’re perfect, a lot of sick folks are going to die. If we will only marry and stay married to perfect spouses, we’re going to be alone a very long time.

Likewise, we need to deal with the political system we have, not the one we wish we had. We can certainly work to improve the system or change it altogether but abstaining from participation in the meantime when so much is at stake is itself complicit behavior.

Once we get the exact candidate we want, though, once we establish the reforms, laws, and economic systems we want, we can still never let our guard down.

We just got back from the grocery and filled our fridge? Would any of us ever consider that a *final* victory?

In any event, I've said my piece. Everything should be fine now. And it's time for some happily ever after semi-annual maintenance sex with my husband. He seems reluctant to head into the bedroom with me, though I really don't understand why. I bathed last month, didn't I? I'm good.

Books by Johnny Townsend

Thanks for reading! If you enjoyed this book, could you please take a few minutes to write a review online? Reviews are helpful both to me as an author and to other readers, so we'd all sincerely appreciate your writing one! And if you did enjoy the book, here are some others I've written you might want to look up:

Mormon Underwear

God's Gargoyles

The Circumcision of God

Sex among the Saints

Dinosaur Perversions

Zombies for Jesus

The Abominable Gayman

The Gay Mormon Quilter's Club

The Golem of Rabbi Loew

Mormon Fairy Tales

Flying over Babel

Marginal Mormons

Mormon Bullies

The Mormon Victorian Society

Dragons of the Book of Mormon

Selling the City of Enoch

A Day at the Temple

Behind the Zion Curtain

Gayrabian Nights

Lying for the Lord

Despots of Deseret

Missionaries Make the Best Companions

Invasion of the Spirit Snatchers

The Tyranny of Silence

Sex on the Sabbath

The Washing of Brains

The Mormon Inquisition

Interview with a Mission President

Weeping, Wailing, and Gnashing of Teeth

Behind the Bishop's Door

The Moat around Zion

The Last Days Linger

Mormon Madness

Human Compassion for Beginners

Dead Mankind Walking

Who Invited You to the Orgy?

Breaking the Promise of the Promised Land

I Will, Through the Veil

Am I My Planet's Keeper?

Have Your Cum and Eat It, Too

Strangers with Benefits

What Would Anne Frank Do?

This Is All Just Too Hard

Glory to the Glory Hole!

My Pre-Bucket List

Blessed Are the Firefighters

Wake Up and Smell the Missionaries

Quilting Beyond the Rainbow

Gay Sleeping Arrangements

Racism by Proxy

Orgy at the STD Clinic

Life Is Better with Love

Please Evacuate

Recommended Daily Humanity

The Camper Killings

Let the Faggots Burn: The UpStairs Lounge Fire

Latter-Gay Saints: An Anthology of Gay Mormon Fiction (co-editor)

Available from your favorite online or neighborhood bookstore.

Wondering what some of those other books are about? Read on!

Invasion of the Spirit Snatchers

During the Apocalypse, a group of Mormon survivors in Hurricane, Utah gather in the home of the Relief Society president, telling stories to pass the time as they ration their food storage and await the Second Coming. But this is no ordinary group of Mormons—or perhaps it is. They are the faithful, feminist, gay, apostate, and repentant, all working together to help each other through the darkest days any of them have yet seen.

Gayrabian Nights

Gayrabian Nights is a twist on the well-known classic, *1001 Arabian Nights*, in which Scheherazade, under the threat of death if she ceases to captivate King Shahryar's attention, enchants him through a series of mysterious, adventurous, and romantic tales.

In this variation, a male escort, invited to the hotel room of a closeted, homophobic Mormon senator, learns that the man is poised to vote on a piece of anti-gay legislation the following morning. To prevent him from sleeping, so that the exhausted senator will miss casting his vote on the Senate floor, the escort entertains him with stories of homophobia, celibacy, mixed orientation marriages, reparative therapy, coming out, first love, gay marriage, and long-term successful gay relationships. The escort crafts the stories to give the senator a crash course in gay culture and sensibilities, hoping to bring the man closer to accepting his own sexual orientation.

Let the Faggots Burn: The UpStairs Lounge Fire

On Gay Pride Day in 1973, someone set the entrance to a French Quarter gay bar on fire. In the terrible inferno that followed, thirty-two people lost their lives, including a third of the local congregation of the Metropolitan Community Church, their pastor burning to death halfway out a second-story window as he tried to claw his way to freedom. A mother who'd gone to the bar with her two gay sons died alongside them. A man who'd helped his friend escape first was found dead near the fire escape. Two children waited outside a movie theater across town for a father and stepfather who would never pick them up. During this era of rampant homophobia, several families refused to claim the bodies, and many churches refused to bury the dead. Author Johnny Townsend pored through old records and tracked down survivors of the fire as well as relatives and friends of those killed to compile this fascinating account of a forgotten moment in gay history.

The Abominable Gayman

What is a gay Mormon missionary doing in Italy? He is trying to save his own soul as well as the souls of others. In these tales chronicling the two-year mission of Robert Anderson, we see a young man tormented by his inability to be the man the Church says he should be. In addition to his personal hell, Anderson faces a major earthquake, organized crime, a serious bus accident, and much more. He copes with horrendous mission leaders and his own suicidal tendencies. But one day, he meets another missionary who loves him, and his world changes forever.

Marginal Mormons

What happens when a High Priest becomes addicted to crack cocaine? Do gay people have positive near-death experiences or unhappy ones? Is there a way to splice the empathy gene into the genome of every human? Can a schizophrenic woman on anti-delusional drugs still keep her belief in an intangible God? Will a childless biochemist be able to find fulfillment by taking part in a mission to Mars? Not every Latter-day Saint has a mainstream story to tell, but these soul-searching people are still more than the marginal Mormons headquarters would like us to believe.

Missionaries Make the Best Companions

What lies behind the freshly scrubbed façades of the Mormon missionaries we see about town? In these stories, an ex-Mormon tries to seduce a faithful elder by showing him increasingly suggestive movies. A sister missionary fulfills her community service requirement by babysitting for a prostitute. Two elders break their mission rules by venturing into the forbidden French Quarter. A senior missionary couple try to reactivate lapsed members while their own family falls apart back home. A young man hopes that serving a second full-time mission will lead him up the Church hierarchy. Two bored missionaries decide to make a little extra money moonlighting in a male stripper club. Two frustrated elders find an acceptable way to masturbate—by donating to a Fertility Clinic. A lonely man searches for the favorite companion he hasn't seen in thirty years.

The Last Days Linger

The scriptures tell us that in the Last Days, wickedness will increase upon the Earth. When leaders of the Mormon Church see a rise in the number of gay members, they believe the end is upon them. But while "wickedness never was happiness," it begins to appear that wickedness can sometimes be divine. At least, the stories here suggest that religious proscriptions condemning homosexuality have it all wrong. While gay Mormons may be no closer to perfection than anyone else, they're no further from it, either. And sometimes, being gay provides just the right ingredient to create saints—as flawed as God himself.

Mormon Madness

Mental illness can strike the faithful as easily as anyone else. But often religious doctrine and practice exacerbate rather than alleviate these problems. From schizophrenia to obsessive-compulsive disorder, from persecution complex to sexual dysfunction, autism to dissociative identity disorder, Mormons must cope with their mental as well as their spiritual health on a daily basis.

Breaking the Promise of the Promised Land: How Religious Conservatives Failed America

By aligning themselves over the past 60 years with the most conservative wing of the Republican Party, Mormons became leading contributors to the cultural and moral decay of America. Mormon prophets have long declared that God set America apart for the righteous. It was to be a land of freedom, justice, and peace, a place where the Lamanites could blossom as the rose, a country so righteous that the affairs of the entire world would be conducted here during the Millennium.

But when Mormons tired of being "a peculiar people" and chose to side with the most repressive evangelicals, they chose to make America the land of the imprisoned, poor, and oppressed. While declaring their allegiance to the Prince of Peace, they've chosen to support policies that have kept America at war almost non-stop for the last six decades.

Am I My Planet's Keeper?

Global Warming. Climate Change. Climate Crisis. Climate Emergency. Whatever label we use, we are facing one of the greatest challenges to the survival of life as we know it.

But while addressing greenhouse gases is perhaps our most urgent need, it's not our only task. We must also address toxic waste, pollution, habitat destruction, and our other contributions to the world's sixth mass extinction event.

In order to do that, we must simultaneously address the unmet human needs that keep us distracted from deeper engagement in stabilizing our climate: moderating economic inequality, guaranteeing healthcare to all, and ensuring education for everyone.

And to accomplish *that*, we must unite to combat the monied forces that use fear, prejudice, and misinformation to manipulate us.

It's a daunting task. But success is our only option.

Wake Up and Smell the Missionaries

Two Mormon missionaries in Italy discover they share the same rare ability—both can emit pheromones on demand. At first, they playfully compete in the hills of Frascati to see who can tempt "investigators" most. But soon they're targeting each other non-stop.

Can two immature young men learn to control their "superpower" to live a normal life… and develop genuine love? Even as their relationship is threatened by the attentions of another man?

They seem just on the verge of success when a massive earthquake leaves them trapped under the rubble of their apartment in Castellammare.

With night falling and temperatures dropping, can they dig themselves out in time to save themselves? And will their injuries destroy the ability that brought them together in the first place?

Racism by Proxy

Are you biased? Am I?

The short answer is yes. We all are.

Having bias isn't a choice. We can't avoid it. We prefer members of our religion, our country, our political party, and speakers of our native language.

We're taught bias by people who aren't conscious of their biases, and we in turn unintentionally pass them on to others.

So it's not a "sin" to be biased. It's inevitable.

What matters is not allowing our unchosen biases to exert absolute control over our decisions and behavior.

To do that, however, we must recognize and accept them as real.

In *Racism by Proxy*, essayist Johnny Townsend pushes past shame, guilt, insults, and other useless approaches to show how all of us, even white people of varying privilege, benefit from increasing equity and social justice throughout our communities.

Orgy at the STD Clinic

Todd Tillotson is struggling to move on after his husband is killed in a hit and run attack a year earlier during a Black Lives Matter protest in Seattle.

In this novel set entirely on public transportation, we watch as Todd, isolated throughout the pandemic, battles desperation in his attempt to safely reconnect with the world.

Will he find love again, even casual friendship, or will he simply end up another crazy old man on the bus?

Things don't look good until a man whose face he can't even see sits down beside him despite the raging variants.

And asks him a question that will change his life.

Please Evacuate

A gay, partygoing New Yorker unconcerned about the future or the unsustainability of capitalism is hit by a truck and thrust into a straight man's body half a continent away. As Hunter tries to figure out what's happening, he's caught up in another disaster, a wildfire sweeping through a Colorado community, the flames overtaking him and several schoolchildren as they flee.

When he awakens, Hunter finds himself in the body of yet another man, this time in northern Italy, a former missionary about to marry a young Mormon woman. Still piecing together this new reality, and beginning to embrace his latest identity, Hunter fights for his life in a devastating flash flood along with his wife *and* his new husband.

He's an aging worker in drought-stricken Texas, a nurse at an assisted living facility in the direct path of a hurricane, an advocate for the unhoused during a freak Seattle blizzard.

We watch as Hunter is plunged into life after life, finally recognizing the futility of only looking out for #1 and understanding the part he must play in addressing the global climate crisis…if he ever gets another chance.

Recommended Daily Humanity

A checklist of human rights must include basic housing, universal healthcare, equitable funding for public schools, and tuition-free college and vocational training.

In addition to the basics, though, we need much more to fully thrive. Subsidized childcare, universal pre-K, a universal basic income, subsidized high-speed internet, net neutrality, fare-free public transit (plus *more* public transit), and medically assisted death for the terminally ill who want it.

None of this will matter, though, if we neglect to address the rapidly worsening climate crisis.

Sound expensive? It is.

But not as expensive as refusing to implement these changes. The cost of climate disasters each year has grown to staggering figures. And the cost of social and political upheaval from not meeting the needs of suffering workers, families, and individuals may surpass even that.

It's best we understand that the vast sums required to enact meaningful change are an investment which will pay off not only in some indeterminate future but in fact almost immediately. And without these adjustments to our lifestyles and values, there may very well not be a future capable of sustaining freedom and democracy…or even civilization itself.

What Readers Have Said

Townsend's stories are "a gay *Portnoy's Complaint* of Mormonism. Salacious, sweet, sad, insightful, insulting, religiously ethnic, quirky-faithful, and funny."

D. Michael Quinn, author of *The Mormon Hierarchy: Origins of Power*

"Told from a believably conversational first-person perspective, [*The Abominable Gayman*'s] novelistic focus on Anderson's journey to thoughtful self-acceptance allows for greater character development than often seen in short stories, which makes this well-paced work rich and satisfying, and one of Townsend's strongest. An extremely important contribution to the field of Mormon fiction." Named to Kirkus Reviews' Best of 2011.

Kirkus Reviews

"The thirteen stories in *Mormon Underwear* capture this struggle [between Mormonism and homosexuality] with humor, sadness, insight, and sometimes shocking details… *Mormon Underwear* provides compelling stories, literally from the inside-out."

Niki D'Andrea, *Phoenix New Times*

"Townsend's lively writing style and engaging characters [in *Zombies for Jesus*] make for stories which force us to wake up, smell the (prohibited) coffee, and review our attitudes with regard to reading dogma so doggedly. These are tales which revel in the individual tics and quirks which make us human, Mormon or not, gay or not…"

A.J. Kirby, The Short Review

"The Rift," from *The Abominable Gayman*, is a "fascinating tale of an untenable situation… a *tour de force*."

David Lenson, editor, *The Massachusetts Review*

"Pronouncing the Apostrophe," from *The Golem of Rabbi Loew*, is "quiet and revealing, an intriguing tale…"

Sima Rabinowitz, Literary Magazine Review, NewPages.com

The Circumcision of God is "a collection of short stories that consider the imperfect, silenced majority of Mormons, who may in fact be [the Church's] best hope… [The book leaves] readers regretting the church's willingness to marginalize those who best exemplify its ideals: those who love fiercely despite all obstacles, who brave challenges at great personal risk and who always choose the hard, higher road."

Kirkus Reviews

In *Mormon Fairy Tales*, Johnny Townsend displays "both a wicked sense of irony and a deep well of compassion."

Kel Munger, *Sacramento News and Review*

Zombies for Jesus is "eerie, erotic, and magical."

Publishers Weekly

"While [Townsend's] many touching vignettes draw deeply from Mormon mythology, history, spirituality and culture, [*Mormon Fairy Tales*] is neither a gaudy act of proselytism nor angry protest literature from an ex-believer. Like all good fiction, his stories are simply about the joys, the hopes and the sorrows of people."

Kirkus Reviews

"In *Let the Faggots Burn* author Johnny Townsend restores this tragic event [the UpStairs Lounge fire] to its proper place in LGBT history and reminds us that the victims of the blaze were not just 'statistics,' but real people with real lives, families, and friends."

Jesse Monteagudo, The Bilerico Project

In *Let the Faggots Burn*, "Townsend's heart-rending descriptions of the victims… seem to [make them] come alive once more."

Kit Van Cleave, *OutSmart Magazine*

Marginal Mormons is "an irreverent, honest look at life outside the mainstream Mormon Church… Throughout his musings on sin and forgiveness, Townsend beautifully demonstrates his characters' internal, perhaps irreconcilable struggles… Rather than anger and disdain, he offers an honest portrayal of people searching for meaning and community in their lives, regardless of their life choices or secrets." Named to Kirkus Reviews' Best of 2012.

Kirkus Reviews

The stories in *The Mormon Victorian Society* "register the new openness and confidence of gay life in the age of same-sex marriage… What hasn't changed is Townsend's wry, conversational prose, his subtle evocations of character and social dynamics, and his deadpan humor. His warm empathy still glows in this intimate yet clear-eyed engagement with Mormon theology and folkways. Funny, shrewd and finely wrought dissections of the awkward contradictions—and surprising harmonies—between conscience and desire." Named to Kirkus Reviews' Best of 2013.

Kirkus Reviews

"This collection of short stories [*The Mormon Victorian Society*] featuring gay Mormon characters slammed [me] in the face from the first page, wrestled my heart and mind to the floor, and left me panting and wanting more by the end. Johnny Townsend has created so many memorable characters in such few pages. I went weeks thinking about this book. It truly touched me."

Tom Webb, A Bear on Books

Dragons of the Book of Mormon is an "entertaining collection… Townsend's prose is sharp, clear, and easy to read, and his characters are well rendered…"

Publishers Weekly

"The pre-eminent documenter of alternative Mormon lifestyles… Townsend has a deep understanding of his characters, and his limpid prose, dry humor and well-grounded (occasionally magical) realism make their spiritual conundrums both compelling and entertaining. [*Dragons of the Book of Mormon* is] [a]nother of Townsend's critical but affectionate and absorbing tours of Mormon discontent." Named to Kirkus Reviews' Best of 2014.

Kirkus Reviews

In *Gayrabian Nights*, "Townsend's prose is always limpid and evocative, and… he finds real drama and emotional depth in the most ordinary of lives."

Kirkus Reviews

Gayrabian Nights is a "complex revelation of how seriously soul damaging the denial of the true self can be."

Ryan Rhodes, author of *Free Electricity*

Gayrabian Nights "was easily the most original book I've read all year. Funny, touching, topical, and thoroughly enjoyable."

Rainbow Awards

Lying for the Lord is "one of the most gripping books that I've picked up for quite a while. I love the author's writing style, alternately cynical, humorous, biting, scathing, poignant, and touching.... This is the third book of his that I've read, and all are equally engaging. These are stories that need to be told, and the author does it in just the right way."

Heidi Alsop, Ex-Mormon Foundation Board Member

In *Lying for the Lord*, Townsend "gets under the skin of his characters to reveal their complexity and conflicts... shrewd, evocative [and] wryly humorous."

Kirkus Reviews

In *Missionaries Make the Best Companions*, "the author treats the clash between religious dogma and liberal humanism with vivid realism, sly humor, and subtle feeling as his characters try to figure out their true missions in life. Another of Townsend's rich dissections of Mormon failures and uncertainties..." Named to Kirkus Reviews' Best of 2015.

Kirkus Reviews

In *Invasion of the Spirit Snatchers*, "Townsend, a confident and practiced storyteller, skewers the hypocrisies and eccentricities of his characters with precision and affection. The outlandish framing narrative is the most consistent source of shock and humor, but the stories do much to ground the reader in the world—or former world—of the characters... A funny, charming tale about a group of Mormons facing the end of the world."

Kirkus Reviews

"Townsend's collection [*The Washing of Brains*] once again displays his limpid, naturalistic prose, skillful narrative chops, and his subtle insights into psychology... Well-crafted dispatches on the clash between religion and self-fulfillment..."

Kirkus Reviews

"While the author is generally at his best when working as a satirist, there are some fine, understated touches in these tales [*The Last Days Linger*] that will likely affect readers in subtle ways... readers should come away impressed by the deep empathy he shows for all his characters—even the homophobic ones."

Kirkus Reviews

"Written in a conversational style that often uses stories and personal anecdotes to reveal larger truths, this immensely approachable book [*Racism by Proxy*] skillfully serves its intended audience of White readers grappling with complex questions regarding race, history, and identity. The author's frequent references to the Church of Jesus Christ of Latter-day Saints may be too niche for readers unfamiliar with its idiosyncrasies, but Townsend generally strikes a perfect balance of humor, introspection, and reasoned arguments that will engage even skeptical readers."

Kirkus Reviews

Orgy at the STD Clinic portrays "an all-too real scenario that Townsend skewers to wincingly accurate proportions…[with] instant classic moments courtesy of his punchy, sassy, sexy lead character…"

Jim Piechota, *Bay Area Reporter*

Orgy at the STD Clinic is "…a triumph of humane sensibility. A richly textured saga that brilliantly captures the fraying social fabric of contemporary life." Named to Kirkus Reviews' Best Indie Books of 2022.

Kirkus Reviews

Acknowledgment of Prior Publication

"All or Nothing Racism," published in *What Would Anne Frank Do?* BookLocker.com, June 2020

"Ban All Routine Traffic Stops," published in *LA Progressive* on 30 May 2020

"Before Things Turned Violent," published in *Resistance: DoveTales, an International Journal of the Arts*, Summer 2020 issue III

"Beheading Rats, Harassing Women, and Making Artificial Cerebrospinal Fluid," published in *Blessed Are the Firefighters*, BookLocker.com, Feb 2021

"Better Off Dead," published in *LA Progressive* on 14 April 2021

"Cages, Camps, Jails, and Prisons," published in *Breaking the Promised of the Promised Land,* BookLocker.com, Sept 2019

"Chimney Sweeps, Typesetters, Tobacco Farmers, and the Police," published in *LA Progressive* on 13 June 2020

"Church Courses to Overcome Unconscious Bias," published in *LA Progressive* on 9 April 2021

"Deadnaming our Military Bases," published in *LA Progressive* on 21 June 2020

"Don't Feed the Humans: Criminalizing Compassion," published in the *Orlando Sentinel* on 18 June 2019

"Do We See the Person in 'Homeless Person'?" published in *Am I My Planet's Keeper?* BookLocker.com, Feb 2020

"Exposure Isn't Enough," published in *LA Progressive* on 1 April 2021

"Facing our Biases without Self-Loathing," published in *LA Progressive* on 8 July 2020

"First Responders: Police, Firefighters, and… Mental Health Officers?" published in *LA Progressive* on 27 December 2020

"Go and Sin a Little Less," published in *LA Progressive* on 28 March 2021

"Is Critical Race Theory 'True'?" published in the *Salt Lake Tribune* on 3 June 2021

"I Threw My Confederate Cap Away," published in *Flip Sides*, Wising Up Press: Decatur, GA, April 2021. Eds. Charles Brockett and Heather Tosteson

"It's Their Culture I Don't Like," published in *LA Progressive* on 24 April 2021

"Keeping the Pantry Full: Freedom and Justice Demand Constant Vigilance," published in *LA Progressive* on 4 September 2020

"Learn the Truth: Facing Revisionist History," published in *LA Progressive* on 14 May 2021

"Let's Rehearse Anti-Racist Strategies," published in *LA Progressive* on 16 July 2020

"LGBTQ Lit for Mormons," published in the *Salt Lake Tribune*, 2 July 2017

"Make the Apocalypse Great Again," published in the *Salt Lake Tribune* on 4 March 2021

"Mandatory Courses on Race, Gender, and Social Justice," published in *LA Progressive* on 23 Nov 2018

"More Social Justice, Less Civil Disorder," published in *LA Progressive* on 25 July 2020

"Mormons Must Stop Practicing Racism by Proxy," published in the *Salt Lake Tribune* on 19 June 2020

"Mormons Should Make Jesus Semitic Again," published in *Main Street Plaza* on 5 July 2020

"Oh, Say Can You Unsee," published in *LA Progressive* on 31 July 2020

"One-Tenth More Empathy to Create Real Change," published in the *Salt Lake Tribune* on 30 April 2021 and republished in *LA Progressive* on 2 May 2021

"Perfectionists against Self-Improvement," published in *Main Street Plaza* on 12 May 2021

"Prerequisites for a Livable Society," published in *LA Progressive* on 9 May 2021

"Privilege Doesn't Mean Life Is Perfect," published in *What Would Anne Frank Do?* BookLocker.com, June 2020

"Protesting at a Black Lives Matter Rally Revealed More of My Biases," published in *LA Progressive* on 11 June 2020

"Racist Gods," published in *LA Progressive* on 17 March 2021

"Resisting Bigotry One Day at a Time," published in *LA Progressive* on 12 July 2020

"Sex Is Work," published in *Blessed Are the Firefighters*, BookLocker.com, Feb 2021

"Subsidizing Cultural Appreciation," published in *Am I My Planet's Keeper?* BookLocker.com, Feb 2020

"Successful Citizens Are the Key to Beating China and Russia," published in *LA Progressive* on 5 May 2021

"Suppression of Information Is a Human Rights Abuse," published in *LA Progressive* on 5 July 2020.

"That Time I Wasn't Killed by the Police," published in *LA Progressive* on 28 July 2020

"Things to Say to the Police While Being Murdered," published in *What Would Anne Frank Do?* Booklocker.com, June 2020

"To Be an Ally or Not To Be," published in *Breaking the Promise of the Promised Land*, BookLocker.com, Sept 2019

"Train Up a Child in the Bias He Should Know," published in the *Salt Lake Tribune* on 7 August 2020

"Trick-or-Treating with the Homeless," published in *Am I My Planet's Keeper?* BookLocker.com, Feb 2020

"Troll Others and Be the Worse for It," published in *LA Progressive* on 7 May 2021

"Virtue Signaling, Mansplaining, and Whitesplaining," published in *LA Progressive* on 20 June 2020

"When Protesting Genocide Is a Racist Act," published in the *Salt Lake Tribune* on 12 May 2019

"White Racist for Black Lives Matter," published in *LA Progressive* on 22 July 2020

Additional Resources for White Allies

There's far more available than the few items listed below. This short list is just to offer a few starting options. I've included many items about oppression in general, as all forms work to divide allies, and solidarity with others is the best way forward.

Race (Black):

"4 Little Girls" (documentary about the Birmingham church bombing that killed four girls)

"Africa's Great Civilizations" (PBS documentary featuring Henry Gates, debunking myths about Africa)

"American Experience—Freedom Riders" (PBS documentary of civil rights movement in the 1960s)

"American Experience—Scottsboro: An American Tragedy" (PBS documentary of the legal battle from 1931 that gave birth to the civil rights movement)

"Black Panthers: Vanguard of the Revolution" (PBS documentary)

"The Central Park Five" (PBS documentary about the wrongful incarceration of five Black and Latino teens who are eventually freed after the real rapist's confession)

"Dark Girls" (documentary about discrimination based on varying shades of dark skin)

"Dreamland: The Burning of Black Wall Street" (documentary)

"Driving While Black" (PBS documentary)

"Finding Your Roots" (almost any episode of this PBS series featuring a Black guest will do: Epatha Merkerson discovers the sale of her ancestor was directly related to the survival of Georgetown University, Questlove learns that his ancestor came on the very last slave ship to the US, Gloria Reuben discovers her ancestor who came from Africa on the Middle Passage in 1817, country singer Roseanne Carter Cash learns that she has African ancestry on both sides of her family, and Wanda Sykes, Michael Strahan, Maya Rudolph, John Legend, and many others have fascinating histories that help viewers understand the enormity of the impact "history" still has on the lives of Black Americans today)

"Hair Story: Untangling the Roots of Black Hair in America" (book by Ayanna Byrd that details the many ways Black hair is used to discriminate at school, in the workplace, and elsewhere)

"The Hate U Give" (fictionalized story about a teen who witnesses an unprovoked police killing)

"I am not your Negro" (documentary about novelist James Baldwin)

"If Beale Street Could Talk" (film adaptation of a James Baldwin novel about a young couple in Harlem, the young woman fighting to prove her husband's innocence)

"Just Mercy" (fictionalized account of the true story of an attorney fighting racism in the criminal justice system)

"Let the Fire Burn" (documentary covering the police attack on MOVE, a Black power group, leading to the death of 11 people and the destruction of 61 homes)

"March" (trilogy of graphic novels about the civil rights movement)

"Racially Charged: America's Misdemeanor Problem" (short documentary by Brave New Films)

"Reconstruction: America after the Civil War" (PBS documentary)

"Reparations: A Christian Call for Repentance and Repair" (book by two evangelical Christians—one white and one Asian—calling for Christians to come with a working plan for reparations)

"Secrets of the Dead: America's Untold Story" (PBS documentary, 4 parts, revealing overlooked history including slave escapes to a free Florida in the 1700s, the first free Black settlement in America, how free Blacks and Native Americans worked together in St. Augustine and other locales, before the U.S. took over Florida)

"Selma" (fictionalized account of the march in Selma)

"Slavery by Another Name" (PBS documentary showing how the laws were manipulated to continue enslaving Blacks after the end of the Civil War)

"Slavery and the Making of America" (PBS documentary showing some of the history)

"Spies of Mississippi" (PBS documentary about anti-civil rights spies trying to undermine the civil rights movement)

"Trial of the Chicago 7" (Fictionalized account of the trial after the riots in Chicago during the 1968 Democratic National Convention. It shows how an 8th defendant, a Black man, received NO attorney representation and was physically gagged when he complained. Also includes info about the Black Panthers.)

"Tulsa, 1921: Reporting a Massacre" (book by Randy Krehbiel and Karlos Hill about the destruction of "Black Wall Street" and murder of at least 300 in a white supremacist attack)

"The Tuskegee Airmen" (PBS documentary about a group of African American fighter pilots during WWII)

"Underground Railroad: The William Still Story" (PBS documentary)

"Wilmington's Lie: The Murderous Coup of 1898 and the Rise of White Supremacy" (Pultizer Prize winner David Zucchino's account of white supremacists overthrowing an elected government, murdering at least 60 Black men in the process)

Race (Native American):

"Beans" (feature film based on the 78-day standoff between a Mohawk community and the government of Quebec, winner of Canadian Screen Award)

"Biography: Sitting Bull, Chief of the Lakota Nation" (documentary)

"Exterminate All the Brutes" (HBO documentary on white supremacy, covering 500 years of U.S. history)

"Geronimo and the Apache Resistance" (documentary)

"The Great Indian Wars 1540-1890" (documentary)

"House Made of Dawn" (Pulitzer-prize winning novel by N. Scott Momaday)

"In Search of History: Navajo Code Talkers" (documentary by The History Channel about the only unbreakable military code, developed by Navajo Marines)

"Life on the Rez" (long news report by Lisa Ling)

"Native America" (PBS documentary about indigenous peoples of the Americas)

"Our Spirits Don't Speak English: Indian Boarding School" (documentary about forced boarding schools for Native Americans to wipe out their cultures and languages)

"Reel Injun" (documentary analyzing the depiction of Native Americans in film)

"Smoke Signals" (fictionalized account of Pacific Northwest indigenous friends)

"Trail of Tears" (documentary about forced relocation of Native Americans)

"We Shall Remain: America Through Native Eyes" (PBS documentary about Native Americans)

"Wind River" (film about missing and murdered Indigenous women, and how conflicts over jurisdiction make this a catastrophic and largely ignored problem)

Race (Asian American):

"The Big Sick" (feature film based on the true story of a Pakistani American comic's awkward relationship with his white girlfriend's parents when she falls into a coma)

"The Chinese Exclusion Act" (PBS documentary about U.S. refusal to accept Chinese immigrants for over 60 years)

"The Karate Kid" (feature film about a bullied teen who is taught karate by a Japanese neighbor and who learns more about Japanese culture through their friendship)

"London River" (feature film about a white British Christian woman and a Black French Muslim man searching for their children after a terrorist attack in 2005)

"They Called Us Enemy" (graphic novel by Star Trek actor George Takei, recounting his time in a Japanese American internment camp)

"Time of Fear" (PBS documentary about Japanese American internment camps during WWII)

"The Wedding Banquet" (feature film about an Asian American gay man in a committed gay relationship who pretends to marry a woman to please his parents visiting from Taiwan)

ADA/Disabilities:

"37 Seconds" (Japanese actor with cerebral palsy portrays an artist who wants to find a career drawing manga)

"Atypical" (Netflix series about a teen with autism)

"The Best Years of Our Lives" (feature film that won several Oscars, set immediately after WWII, starring a man who'd lost both hands in the war)

"Children of a Lesser God" (feature film about a deaf woman, played by Marlee Matlin, the only deaf actress so far to win an Oscar)(she's also acted in several other shows and films, if folks want to see more stories with deaf characters)

"Crip Camp: A Disability Revolution" (Shows the development of the activism leading to the passage of the ADA. Helps us understand the physical obstacles and emotional disregard millions of folks must endure. Includes a powerful scene showing disabled folks literally crawling up the steps of the Capitol to demonstrate the lack of accessibility.)

"Elephant Man" (fictionalized account of the true story of a badly disfigured man who was treated as a circus animal until rescued by a doctor)

"Mask" (feature film starring Cher playing a mother whose son was born disfigured)

"Murderball" (documentary about athletes who play wheelchair rugby)

"The Punk Syndrome" (documentary about a punk rock band whose members are all mentally impaired)

"Shallow Hal" (Primarily about a man who learns to see the inner beauty of others, mostly in terms of obesity and looks, but it also showcases a disabled actor in a supporting role.)

"Sound of Metal" (Oscar-winning film about a heavy metal drummer who begins to lose his hearing)

"Spencer2TheWest" (YouTube channel hosted by a man whose legs were amputated when he was a child, explaining how he drives, swims, goes to the bathroom, etc.)

"Temple Grandin" (feature film about a woman with autism who succeeds as a scientist)

"The Upside" (feature film about a quadriplegic white man who hires a Black ex-con to assist him)

"What You Think I'm Thinking" (A short film, 12 minutes. Featuring a severely disfigured Black burn survivor who goes on his first date since the accident.)

"Wonder" (feature film starring Julia Roberts and Owen Wilson, about a young boy with facial abnormalities making friends at school)

Judaism/Islam:

"The Chosen" (feature film based on a novel by Chaim Potok about the friendship between an Orthodox Jew and a Hassidic Jew, showing that there are many sects among Jews. They aren't a single religion.)

"Fiddler on the Roof" (musical about a poor Jewish milkman whose daughters break tradition by choosing their own husbands)

"The Kite Runner" (film based on the novel about an Afghani immigrant living in California who visits an old friend in Pakistan he'd been too scared to help during an assault years earlier)

"The Life Ahead" (Netflix movie starring Sophia Loren as a Holocaust survivor in Italy taking in a young Muslim orphan from Senegal)

"Schindler's List" (feature film by Steven Spielberg telling the true story of a complicated war criminal who still saves 1200 Jews during the Holocaust)

"Train of Life" (French film about an Eastern European Jewish community during the Holocaust who try to escape by stealing a train and pretending to be a transport to the death camps)

"Two Strangers Who Meet Five Times" (award-winning short film, 12 minutes, by Marcus Markou, about a white racist and a Muslim whose chance encounters change their lives)

"Unorthodox" (Netflix series about a young woman who breaks away from an ultra-Orthodox Jewish community)

"Yentl" (musical starring Barbra Streisand as a woman in Eastern Europe who disguises herself as a man so she can study Talmud)

Gender:

"The Accused" (Jodie Foster won an Oscar for her role. The film accepts the usual accusations thrown at rape victims—she was drunk and high, she was dressed provocatively, she was flirting with the rapist—and shows that none of that justifies or excuses the assault)

"American Experience: The Codebreaker" (PBS documentary about Elizebeth Smith Friedman, whose codebreaking skills helped bring down a Nazi spy ring during WWII, gangsters, and others)

"American Experience: The Vote" (PBS documentary, 2 parts, showing the long struggle of women to win the right to vote)

"Erin Brockovitch" (Fictionalized true story of an impoverished single mom who takes her entry level job and gathers evidence of Pacific Gas and Electric poisoning water, winning compensation for the survivors)

"He Named Me Malala" (documentary about a young woman fighting for the right of girls to be educated, who is shot in the head but survives and eventually wins the Nobel Peace Prize)

"Made in Dagenham" (Fictionalized true story of women auto workers in the UK fighting for equal pay.)

"Suffragette" (Fictionalized account of women winning the right to vote)

LGBTQ:

"The Celluloid Closet" (analyzes depictions of LGBTQ folks in film from silent movies to the present day)

"Disclosure" (Interviews with trans folks, many of them POC, discussing the importance of representation)

"Kinky Boots" (feature film telling the true story of a failing shoe manufacturer who revitalizes his company by making boots for drag queens)

"Let the Record Show" (book by Sarah Schulman about the history of ACT UP, an AIDS protest group)

"Mass Appeal" (The story of an alcoholic priest and a bisexual seminarian who stand up for each other. Stars Jack Lemmon.)

"Pride" (feature film about a group of LGBTQ activists in the UK who raise funds for striking coal miners who don't like them)

"The Times of Harvey Milk" (documentary about the first openly gay elected official in the US)

Social Justice/Labor:

"American Experience: Civilian Conservation Corps" (PBS documentary on this government labor program during the Great Depression)

"American Experience: Triangle Fire" (PBS documentary about horrific working conditions in a New York factory that led to the deaths of 146 employees, mostly young women locked inside a burning building, and the labor reforms that resulted from the disaster)

"Five Past Midnight in Bhopal: The Epic Story of the World's Worst Industrial Disaster" (book by Dominique Lapierre and Javier Moro about lax safety protocols leading to the death of roughly 15,000 people during a leak of poison gas)

"The Hamlet Fire: A Tragic Story of Cheap Food, Cheap Government, and Cheap Lives" (book about how economically depressed townspeople are forced to take dangerous, low-paying jobs)

"Invisible People" (YouTube channel featuring interviews with homeless people)

"Mine Wars" (documentary about oppression of miners)

"Prisons Make Us Safer: And 20 Other Myths About Mass Incarceration" (book by Victoria Law)

"Radium Girls" (feature film about real-life hazardous working conditions that killed workers)

"The Unexpected Guest: How a Homeless Man from the Streets of L.A. Redefined Our Home" (book by Michael Konik detailing how he and his wife took in a homeless man for several months)

www.ingramcontent.com/pod-product-compliance
Lightning Source LLC
Chambersburg PA
CBHW032048020426
42335CB00011B/238

* 9 7 9 8 9 8 7 7 1 1 3 3 0 *